Norfolk's Ch[ ]
Great and Small

PHOTOGRAPHED BY
RICHARD TILBROOK
DESCRIBED BY
CV ROBERTS

JARROLD
PUBLISHING

Contents

ISBN 0-7117-0961-0

Photographs copyright © Richard Tilbrook 1997   Text copyright © C V Roberts 1997
Published by Jarrold Publishing, Norwich 1997   Printed in Great Britain by Jarrold Bookprint Ltd 1997

Preface by the Rt Rev Peter Nott, Bishop of Norwich

The landscape of Norfolk, which has drawn artists through the centuries, is typified by the grandeur of its skies and the presence everywhere of churches – more here per acre than anywhere else in the world. The medieval churches of Norfolk are one of the nation's greatest treasures, not only in the beauty of their architecture, but in the stories they tell of the history of the communities they serve and of the faith to which they bear witness.

Richard Tilbrook's marvellous photographs, composed with an artist's eye, illustrate this rich heritage which, together with Charles Roberts' evocative text, provide an entirely new approach to our churches. These buildings have stood for many centuries but they have not remained unchanged. This book catalogues some of the developments which have taken place, from Medieval to Victorian, and so provides fresh insight into the changing architectural and theological tastes of our forefathers.

The authors bring not only their widely acknowledged expertise and knowledge to this subject, but also their deep love for the churches of Norfolk which is infectious. Their aim is not merely to illustrate, in word and picture, the buildings of the past, but rather to encourage you, the reader, to explore them for yourself, and to discover some of the treasures which are so easily overlooked. There can be few better companions to such an exploration than this book, which is a delight to read and fascinating guide to use.

+ Peter Norvic:

Hingham St Andrew map ref. G7

The tower of St Andrew's is seen from afar, soaring splendidly against the skyline. Drive into Hingham on a sunny day and you have the essential spirit of an old English village – a noble church, with a neighbourly surround of gracious old houses, and a broad village green. What is special about this church is that it was all built of-a-piece in the lushest expression of the **Decorated** style of architecture of the first half of the 14th century. That was the style which, in large measure, came to an abrupt end in 1349-50, when the great plague, the Black Death, destroyed half the population of Norfolk. But here building is said to have gone on for up to another decade after the catastrophe. The interior is superb and awesomely high and spacious. But much more intimate is a restrained wall monument in the north aisle which bears the following inscription:

*In this parish for many generations lived the Lincolns, ancestors of the American
Abraham Lincoln. To him greatest of that lineage many citizens of the United States
of America have erected this memorial in the hope that for all ages between that
land and this land and all lands shall be 'malice towards none with charity for all'*

This last ringing quotation from the American Declaration of Independence makes Hingham St Andrew's very much the American church of Norfolk.

And to the East came three wise men…

**The Story of Saints Felix, Fursey and Cedd, who
brought Christianity to East Anglia, and of the treasury
of churches which grew from their missions.**

WHEN did it all begin, from where did its inspiration come, that wave of Christianity which a handful of saintly men brought to East Anglia in the Dark Ages? From quiet beginnings, the new faith took root here and flourished, and through the passage of 1400 years would bequeath to Norfolk a remarkable treasury of medieval churches, more in number than in any other individual county in England.

In the opening years of the fifth century the Roman legions were pulling out of Britain, called back to defend Rome itself against barbarian invasion. Into the East Anglian breach came mainly Jutish and Frisian settlers from northern Europe, who within a century, by about 500 AD, had effectively colonised this eastern seaboard. The centre of their power was established around Rendlesham in south-east Suffolk where, by about 530, a royal house had sprung up, the Wuffingas. They were an offshoot of the Scyflings, the Royal house of Uppsala.

From among the Wuffingan kings, two names remain firmly in modern memory. First was Radwald, second was his son Sigbert. Radwald it was for whom, when he died in 625 AD, the great Sutton Hoo burial was enacted, providing him with a fine ship and a regal treasure to take him into eternity.

Radwald's influence grew so much that he claimed the title of Bretwalda - King of Britain. Earlier, in Kent, he had been converted to Christianity at the earnest insistence of the King of Kent. But Radwald, one senses, was more a wily politician than a convinced Christian.

Here is the Venerable Bede, in his *Ecclesiastical History of the English Nation*, written at Jarrow in Northumberland and completed in 731, summing up Radwald in a crisp sentence:

'He had long before received Christian baptism in Kent, but to no good purpose, for… he tried to serve both Christ and the ancient gods, and he had in the same shrine an altar for the holy Sacrifice of Christ side by side with a small altar on which victims were offered to devils…'

The Green Man, a face from a past far older than Christianity, is a vibrant pagan survivor who has become absorbed into Christian imagery. This curious example is in Salle church, one of eight or nine churches in the county where you will find him.

*The use of **bold type** in the text indicates that the references highlighted, other than names of churches, will be found in the glossary (pages 110–12).*

Radwald was succeeded by his son Earpwald, who accepted Christianity but, as with father, as with son, to no good purpose, to echo Bede, for soon after his baptism he was murdered by a pagan and 'for three years the province relapsed into heathendom'.

Living in exile in Gaul, meanwhile, was Earpwald's brother Sigbert, or Sigeberht who, according to Bede, had fled there 'to escape the hostility of Radwald'. Now, on his brother's death, he returned to East Anglia. A man of conviction this one, already a devout Christian and a man of learning. No sooner had he taken his crown in 631 than he set about converting his subjects. Overall 'the conversion of the English in the 7th century was a piecemeal affair, carried out by Roman and Irish missions amongst aristocratic circles, as political circumstances allowed' (Kenneth Penn: *The Early Church in Norfolk*). Here in East Anglia the picture was clearer and more concentrated, moulded in particular by two very remarkable and saintly men who would indeed be canonised, Felix and Fursey.

Felix, a French Burgundian, was invited to East Anglia by Sigbert and was established by the king as bishop at Dummoc, traditionally identified as Dunwich, but possibly the Roman shore fort at Walton, near Felixstowe, now disappeared under the sea. Bede again:

'Like a good farmer Felix reaped a rich harvest of believers. He delivered the entire province from its age-old wickedness and infelicity, brought it to the Christian faith and works of righteousness and - in full accord with the significance of his own name - guided it towards eternal felicity'.

For seventeen fruitful years, during which he built many churches - including one on the site now occupied by **Loddon Holy Trinity** - he ruled his bishopric, and died at Dummoc.

Sigbert continued his good works by bringing to his realm the Irish monk, Fursey. He was born 'of noble Irish blood' on the shores of Lough Corrib, in County Galway, in 597, and spent his young years as a monk evangelising around his native land. Passionate and spirited in his faith, he made a vow 'to spend his life as a pilgrim for love of our Lord, and to go wherever God should call him'. That call in good time brought him to East Anglia, and the patronage of King Sigbert, under whose protection he founded a monastery. Again we turn to the Venerable Bede:

'Inspired by the example of Fursey's goodness, many unbelievers were converted to Christ and many who already believed were drawn to greater love and faith in him. Fursey set himself to build a monastery on a site given to him by King Sigbert and to establish a regular observance in it. This monastery was pleasantly situated in some woods close to the sea, within the area of a fortification which the English call Cnobheresburg…'

This Cnobheresburg is generally accepted to be the ancient shore fort of Burgh Castle, but it could well be Caister-on-Sea, where existing Roman walls would have provided an enclosure for the monks against the outside world. Certainly this was the first known monastery in East Anglia. Now we come closer to home, and a feeling of at last being in palpable touch with this distant past. For Fursey might well be called the Apostle of Norfolk, since he is the first named, known missionary to this corner of England. From their monastery near today's Yarmouth (whose site was under the sea in Fursey's day) he and his companions 'travelled through Norfolk, proclaiming the Gospel out of a life totally committed to living it'. Fursey's burning belief - and the expression is apt - is demonstrated in a brief anecdote recorded by Bede, who quotes someone who listened to the saint: 'This informant remembered him describing a vision of fire - and sweating although it was winter'.

To Fursey, all was real. Like the 'renewed attacks of the heathen' on the province at this time, recorded by Bede… though oddly, for the Anglo-Saxon invasions were long since over and the first recorded Viking raid on England - the appalling destruction of the monastery on Lindisfarne - did not come until 793.

Be that as it may, Bede tells us that Fursey foresaw 'that even Monasteries would be endangered'. By now moreover his patron King Sigbert had been killed in battle against the king of Mercia. So Fursey left Norfolk and sailed for Gaul where he was warmly welcomed by King Clovis, who gave him land to build a monastery at Latiniacum (modern Lagny, on the River Marne, east of Paris) where he died four years later.

Back in England, his work seemed secure, for Sigbert was the first of a line of pious East Anglian royalty, including his notable successor King Anna (remembered as the father of the saintly Withburga, who was abbess of the abbey she founded at East Dereham), who protected Christianity and its bishops in their province. The succession list of East Anglia's bishops survives. The see of Dunwich, according to Bede, proceeded from Felix through to Thomas his deacon, then to Boniface and thence to Bisi. Now Bisi, we learn, became too ill to look after his large diocese, so two bishops were annointed in his stead. One stayed at Dunwich, the other set up his see at Elmham.

The evidence points strongly to this being North Elmham, near Dereham, though no contemporary document mentions Elmham as the see for Norfolk until 803. It is now accepted, however, that the pre-conquest remains of a church at **North Elmham** are those of a cathedral. 'Archaeological evidence reveals that it overlays a previous wooden building, and a medieval account of the founding of Norwich Cathedral says that the first cathedral at Elmham was wooden'.

But what of the early churches of this period? They would have been of wood. Who knows how many were destroyed and lost forever when the Viking horror descended on East Anglia about 870, bringing with it the killing - very unpleasantly - of Edmund, king and martyr, near Bury St Edmunds; and the climactic battle at Edington, near the Bristol Channel in 878, when King Alfred halted the advance of the Danes under King Guthrum.

From that event came the Treaty of Wedmore, under which Guthrum was given East Anglia to rule and share among his followers. As recorded in the *Anglo Saxon Chronicle*, this duly happened. Yet it is a curious fact that this region has little or no archaeological traces of the Danes, though their influence is recalled in many place names.

So what surviving buildings from the 7th and 8th centuries do we have in this part of England? For the earliest East Anglian thread, we must go to Essex, where a tiny, remote chapel near Bradwell on Sea is all that remains of the 7th century monastery established by St Cedd, who was

Bishop of the East Saxons from 654 to 664, yet another of the missionary monks brought here by King Sigbert.

Here he built first a wooden church, which was soon rebuilt in stone, largely reused Roman materials. It is still open for worship in summer-time today, an almost continuous thread (for it was long in use for agricultural needs) through fourteen centuries. In its day, when the saint was alive, it was an important centre from which the Word went out all over East Anglia and beyond. Recently a poignant disaster in West Norfolk took us back to the same distant era. For when one night the round flint tower of **Cockley Cley** church collapsed without warning, it served to reveal construction details which may well date it in the 7th century.

We have a goodly number of churches in the county containing Saxon fabric - about fifty is the general agreement, which is more than in any other county. But that doughty champion of our round towers, W J Goode, in his *The Round Tower Churches of South East England*, argues that almost all of Norfolk's round-towered churches (120 standing, eight visible as ruins and twenty-two no longer visible) are Saxon. That, one might suggest, is a debate which will run and run.

At **East Lexham**, near Swaffham, the little church of **St Andrew** - sited now in the middle of a farm, whose owners tend the church lovingly - has a round tower which is odd to behold, massive and almost crude in its rustic construction, and narrowing towards the top.

East Lexham church has what could possibly be the oldest round tower in England, for local belief is that this massive Saxon structure dates from about the year 900.

Newton-by-Castle Acre church of St Andrew is an immensely appealing little place, with a diminutive and delightful Saxon interior. The Saxon tower was given its continental-looking cap much more recently.

It has long been believed locally that it dates from about 900 - which would make it the oldest surviving round tower in the land. Look closely and notice the massive amounts of mortar used between the flints and conglomerate of which it is constructed.

It must have been built in slices, so to speak, to give time for the mortar in each section to set and settle, before it could take the weight of the next stage. How long, one wonders, did the labour take? The tower's only openings from its Saxon beginnings are at belfry level, three in number, one supported by a roughly hewn round pillar, the second by a baluster (a short column, bulging at the middle and tapering at top and bottom) of typically Saxon character; and the third, a bit of a mystery, a massive Maltese cross in lieu of tracery, of unknown date and origin.

If the tower is ancient, its setting is yet older. The site is roughly circular, and surrounded by a still discernible ditch, which suggests a centre of pagan worship here before the coming of Christianity in the 7th century.

From these rural simplicities to grandeur is but a short step: back along a twisting lane to the main Fakenham-Swaffham road, follow that for a short spell (with a stop, surely, at **All Saints, Newton-by-Castle Acre**, an enchanting little place whose tiny Saxon interior is a joy); then off to the right for Castle Acre.

A visit here is always an event. The road threads between picturesque cottages before passing under the castle gate, whose great castle ruins rise

spectacularly to the right. Then into a village square of quiet perfection, at whose far end is the gateway into the immense churchyard in whose centre stands the magnificent church of **Castle Acre St James**.

It's a brave sight, this great building with its imposing **Perpendicular** tower and largely Perpendicular character overall, though facing us from this churchyard vantage are three windows of the earlier (first half of 14th century) **Decorated** period, and lively, flowing examples they are. Move on and look at the east window. Almost certainly the tracery is 19th century. But the mullions - the uprights between the traceries - suggest survivals from this church's early days. Note the slim pencil shafts, punctuated by delicate little ring capitals - they have the feel of late 13th century work of the **Early English** period.

Move round to the south side, and from about that same period dates the **priest's door**. Before the **Reformation**, when Henry VIII broke with Rome and the English Protestant church was born, the **chancel** was the preserve of the priest, so he had his own door. The **nave**, on the other hand, belonged to the people.

To either side of this particular priest's door are bold **Tudor** windows, with flattened arches, topped by thin red Tudor bricks, a typical decoration of this period, which was the final phase of the **Perpendicular** style. Pointing the shape of the flattened arch is a **dripstone** which serves both decorative and practical use - it looks attractive, setting off the window below it; but also pushes rain water away from the window.

Note the outline of the dripstone in this case, following the shape of the window below it: it reminds one of the headdresses worn by noble ladies of the Tudor period, a pointed arch over the forehead and extensions down each side to frame the face. Thus the name given to them in the 19th century - **kennel headdresses**. The window shape and that of the hat cannot be coincidental.

If all this is interesting and intriguing, a closer look at the priest's door opens up still more fascinating conjectures. Immediately above the door's arch is another, much taller outline, long since filled in and ending in what could be a rounded Norman arch.

Was this originally a complete doorway, normal width yet around 14ft high? And if so, what was its purpose?

The possible explanation is both romantic and appealing: that it was created to allow a knight, armoured and mounted on his horse, to ride into the chancel and there receive the blessing of Holy Church. St James's, remember, was part of the mighty complex of castle and Cluniac priory (more of that in a moment) built in the late 11th and 12th centuries.

Move on to the west end of the church, below the great tower, and down below in the valley is a serene view of the ruins of the priory just noted, founded by William de Warenne in 1090, built in resoundingly Norman style, and based on the mother house of the Cluniac order at Cluny, in France.

Continue on round the tower (taking in its majestic four-light west window - that is, divided into four by mullions - of grand **High Perpendicular** character) and pause in the porch. The fine north door has carved coats of arms on shields. They are those of the Earls of Arundel and of Surrey - the latter were the de Warennes, builders of the priory, bringing 900 years of history full circle. Open the door and, against the backdrop of a splendid interior, a magnificent tabernacled **font** cover concentrates the attention. This wonderful example dates from the 15th century, rears 26ft upwards and is crowned by a golden dove - sign of the Holy Spirit - with wings outspread in flight. Nearby, below the tower, is a screen, in which boards bearing the commandments have been re-used. These are **decalogue** boards, whose role is explained in a feature panel on page 92. Up above, on the tower arch, is a **Royal Arms**, of a size to complement the building, for George II and dated 1748. Such Arms have their own history, as is set out in the same feature panel on page 92.

Move down to the east end of the nave, to the **pulpit**. This one is a beauty, of the kind called wine-glass pulpits, since they sit securely on delicate, fluted stems like those of an elegant wine glass. It dates from about 1400, has carvings of tiny angels and, among its decorative paintings, includes images of **The Four Latin Doctors** of the Church.

We have dwelt for some time on this one church because it illustrates much which will be met elsewhere throughout this county of medieval churches. Another which enchantingly fits that purpose is Little Snoring, out in the countryside not far from Fakenham, and as small, intimate and simple as Castle Acre is rich and grand.

Little Snoring St Andrew, within a small span, presents in miniature a quite remarkable textbook in stone of architectural styles through six centuries, from **Saxon** England to the Tudors. It sits on a slight ridge, just separated from its village, so that its outline against a typical Norfolk land and skyscape can have fullest effect. For this is a highly distinctive outline, with its round tower, to which a couple of centuries ago was added a perky cap like a pigeon-cote, off-set from the rest of the building.

St Andrew's has many points of interest and immense appeal (it is one of this writer's especial favourites in Norfolk). But the focus at this moment is its remarkable range of window styles. Starting from just north of the porch, we see **Norman** 'slit' windows, tall and narrow like arrow embrasures in a castle, and placing us in the 12th century - perhaps a hundred years on from the separate Saxo-Norman tower.

At the corner of the church, where it is nearest the tower, the corner edge is built with chunks of stone, thus holding together the flint walls. These are **long and short**, which usually indicates Saxon work - but here probably points to local masons under Norman employers doing what their fathers did!

In the west end there's a lovely window in the **reticulated** style - that is, with delicate, lacey tracery, from the Latin reticulus, a lace bag - which places us within the **Decorated** period of architecture and around the years 1320-30. Move on to the north side: and to a succession of **Norman, Early English** (13th century), **Decorated** (first half of the 14th century), **Perpendicular** (from second half of the 14th century to the end of the 15th century) and **Tudor** (16th century).

I have hazarded elsewhere as to how all this came to be, in so modest and rural a building. The answer could well be that there was never enough money here to make major changes or to rebuild. But at least a bow was made to each new era through minor alterations and additions.

The interior of St Andrew's is cool, calm, delightful in its simplicity, with an **Early English chancel** of about 1250 which is light, uncluttered and, in its own way, memorable. We noted at Castle Acre, on the outside of the east window, those Early English pencil shafts and ring capitals. Here, on the inside of the east window, we see how the same style and technique brings all into a beautiful unity of pattern and composition.

Already, in the two highly contrasted churches visited thus far, a panorama of medieval detail is building. A third, which will add again to the picture, is **St Peter's, Great Walsingham**.

Architecturally, it has the particular virtue of being almost wholly of one period, built around 1330-1340, where the **reticulated** phase of the **Decorated style**, encountered in lovely yet modest form at Little Snoring, is here seen in its glory. St Peter's stands proud on a rise, and is approached towards the east end. It is a distinctive approach, for the chancel lies in romantic ruins - it is known that it was already gone by 1583. But low on the south side of the ruinous walls is a curiosity, a small window opening, only a couple of feet above the ground. This was a **Low Side Window**, a medieval feature whose true use is still matter for debate today.

Look closely at the eastern-most buttress of the church's south aisle. There, at about chest height, incised into the stone, is a small round circle, with lines shooting out from a central hole. This is a **scratch dial** which, says the accepted theory, indicated to the priest the hours of masses and offices (services) in pre-Reformation times.

Stand back and look up to the upper windows, the **clerestory** - pronounced clear-storey, which is exactly what it is: clear glass panes to let the light in. This one is very fine, with its quatrefoil (four leaf) shapes - an essentially **Decorated** period style, but in this instance mostly replaced during the **Perpendicular** period.

The windows of the body of the church are a glory of **reticulated** traceries, with a particularly resplendent example in the west face of the massive tower. There one can see clearly two typical usages of the time: **ogee** cusps - flowing S-shaped tracery, going convex to concave; and **mouchettes** - exotic dagger-like outlines.

Crane your neck and look up. High above, the tower sports some super **gargoyles**, ugly as sin. And that ugliness was entirely intended by medieval sculptors. They accepted that if there was good in the world there was also evil. So up on the church went guardian devils, to keep off their own kind. And if Satan's lot did get through the defences, the gargoyles' practical purpose, of shooting rain water off and away from roofs and tower, could also spit out the Devil!

Inside this tower, by the way, are three amazing survivors - three bells, made in King's Lynn between 1330 and 1350, still in place, and still ringing out to the faithful. In her admirable little volume, *The Reformation in Norfolk Parish Churches*, Susan Yaxley reminds us that in the Middle Ages parishes were keenly proud of their bells, and rang them lustily for festivals and sonorously for funerals.

Bells attracted superstitions too: for example, that their ringing would protect the church tower from lightning.

'The great festival for bell ringing', Susan Yaxley tells us, 'was All Souls, when, either at Hallowmass (November 1st) or All Souls Day (November 2nd) the church bells were rung all night in honour of the souls of the departed. The bell ringers needed a good supply of ale to see them through the night and a collection was often made to pay for this'.

Not surprisingly, Protestant opinion, as Henry VIII's **Reformation** took hold and 'Popish' practices were frowned upon, was pretty firmly against bells - and especially against the hullaballoo and ale-drinking of All Saints.

The south porch is worth a close look. It's good 15th century Perpendicular work, neatly set-off with East Anglian **chequerwork** - knapped (split) flints alternating with stone. Within the porch is a **holy water** stoup, in which holy water was placed so that the faithful might dip in their fingers and cross themselves.

Inside, St Peter's has grace, spaciousness and a lovely atmosphere, as well as much of tremendous interest. Its great treasure is a superb set of

15th century bench pews, with carved ends - including curious carved animals of unknown lineage - whose sculptor clearly had a lively imagination. There's a substantial sill along the floor level of the bench ends. It was a totally practical addition, designed to hold in deep straw which helped keep parishioners' feet warm in winter. On the ends of the north aisle benches are carved images of the disciples, each with his particular symbol - symbols which, with the majority of saints in the calendar, indicate how they were martyred. The number of saints overall is astonishingly large. In Norfolk my own count comes to 108 in wood, glass, paint and stone. On the south aisle wall, very faded now, is a painted cross within a circle. This is a **Consecration Cross** and a bridge through the centuries.

At the east end of the north aisle is a great rarity - an ancient **aumbrey** still fitted with its original door and hinges. Aumbreys were cupboards in which were kept, under lock and key, the sacred vessels of the Mass, and often the Reserved Sacrament. Numerous aumbrey cupboards can be found in Norfolk, but stripped of their doors, locks, hinges and latches. This one is complete.

Now to another subject: tombs. **All Saints at Ashwellthorpe**, near Wymondham, has an intriguing shape as you view it from the road - it seems too high for its modest length, and this is accentuated by the enormous Perpendicular windows of the nave. But it's a pleasing picture nonetheless, with its solid 13th century tower with later battlements of brick and flint chequerwork; 14th century chancel with an 'entertaining' east window, as Nikolaus Pevsner observed in a rare flash of wry humour; and a porch distinguished by having a Dutch gable in brick.

Immediately inside the church is a font which has its own distinctive effect too. It was given by the village's noble Knyvett family in 1660: 'The carving is hard, the date surprising', says Pevsner peremptorily. Certainly it is late for such a gift. But it looks good, standing on a tall shaft, and with its coloured coats of arms around the bowl. Between chancel and north aisle stands Ashwellthorpe's special possession, the rather delightful early 15th century alabaster tomb of Sir Edmund Thorp and his wife Joan. There they lie, the old knight and his lady, gazing heavenwards, and with their hands in prayer. Milady's head, opulently coiffed and bonneted, rests on a pillow which is being smoothed by angels, and little dogs play around her feet. The old warrior, munificently moustached, aptly chooses his helmet for a pillow - after all, he died beside his sovereign, Henry V, during a siege in Normandy in 1417, whence his body was brought home to Ashwellthorpe.

What is especially interesting is that both knight and lady wear the Collar of S's - a gold or silver collar of S's linked together - a signal sign of royal favour. Only a few years before Sir Edmund died, Henry IV limited its use to sons of the king, dukes, earls and barons; and to other knights and esquires when in his presence.

The tomb, in buttery mellow alabaster, is covered with nearly six centuries of idle graffiti. But it is still beautiful.

Beautiful, spectacular and a glorious survivor is the great **rood screen** at **Attleborough's** parish church of the **Assumption of the Blessed Virgin**. It stretches 52ft from wall to wall, across nave and two aisles. Even its **loft** is intact, taking its overall height to about 20ft. It is gloriously colourful and splendid in execution. Above it is a superlative wall painting, of about 1500, showing a richly peopled **Annunciation** scene - when the Archangel Gabriel came to Mary to tell her she would bear the Christ-child.

Norfolk is blessed with many fine screens, but there is not another church in all East Anglia which can match this one for size and completeness.

Given by a local family in 1475, it has weathered centuries of religious change. The story of how it came through, against all the odds, is the stuff of film scripts - and is shared indeed by the church itself which, largely 15th century and big and stately as it is, was once much larger. For the full saga, refer to Mortlock and Roberts in *The Popular Guide to Norfolk Churches*, vol. 3.

All Saints at Bale (between Fakenham and Holt) is largely 14th century, though its lovely chancel is from about 1300. It may not have the splendour of Attleborough, but in considering roods it has a very rare survival indeed. High up at the east end of the nave roof is a pulley-block, whose purpose was to raise and lower the candle beam which lit the rood.

There's some high quality 15th century Norwich stained glass here which repays close attention (Norwich was one of the great centres of the stained glass art at that time).

In the heart of Norfolk's Broadland is **St Michael and All Angels, Barton Turf**. A beautiful building in a lovely country setting, it has a slim and elegant Perpendicular tower of 15th century date (look inside and you'll find there is a fireplace!) and aisles and chancel of the same period. The heart of the church is older, as seen in the nave's arcade arches, though the two late and great authorities on this subject disagree on its date: '13th century', said Munro Cautley; 'early 14th century', said Sir Nikolaus Pevsner firmly.

But enough of that, for one goes to Barton Turf to see its wonderful late 15th century **rood screen** and its paintings of saints and angels. In the late Middle Ages there was a great reverence for angels and here at Barton Turf we have a rare representation of the very ancient Christian doctrine of **The Nine Orders of Angels**. This has its origins in the Old Testament but was first defined and set down about the year 500 by the desert saint, Dionysius the Areopagite.

He classified angels into nine choirs, grouped into three hierarchies. First came the counsellors - seraphim, cherubim, thrones, whose role was to stand in perpetual adoration around the throne of God and receive His glory from Him. Then came the governors of the stars and the elements - dominions, virtues and powers. They receive divine illumination from the first hierarchy and communicate it to the third… but they keep well aloof from mere mortals.

The job of being messengers to us falls to principalities - archangels (Gabriel, Michael and Raphael) and angels, who move between Earth and Heaven.

All nine are seen, gloriously vibrant and colourful, on the Barton Turf screen, together with three female saints, Zita, Apollonia and Barbara. Zita's presence is logical - this pious servant girl of 13th century Italy, the story tells us, was greatly helped by angels. The other two have much more dramatic and violent tales.

In 3rd century Alexandria, poor Apollonia had her teeth torn out by a mob when she refused to renounce her Christianity - and is thus patron saint of dentists and invoked against toothache. She's seen bound to a plank, one thug holding her by the hair while another drags out her molars with vast pincers. Or you may see her, more demurely, holding a tooth in pincers of more sedate size. Look out for her also at **Ludham** and **Norwich St Augustine's.**

Barbara was shut up in a tower by her father in 3rd century Italy when she renounced paganism for Christianity. When she tried to escape her father handed her over to a judge, who ordered her decapitation… whereupon both father and judge were burned to a frazzle by bolts of lightning. Barbara is thus patroness of gunsmiths and artillerymen; and invoked against thunderstorms, lightning and explosions. We shall meet this noisy lady again at **Trunch** and **Edingthorpe**.

Let's move on to **Booton St Michael and All Angels**, which is as individual and eccentric a church as one is likely to meet. The Revd Whitwell Elwin was rector here for fifty years in the 19th century - and spent most of them remodelling and rebuilding his church, pinching designs and ideas from wherever he could find what suited his purpose. And what a purpose.

As you approach it, his zany twin towers at one end of the building attract the slightly startled eye. As you get closer, you find something close to a gothic fantasy, a joyous riot of styles - or the Revd Mr Elwin's version of them - and enough carving, **crockets** and curlicues to humble an exuberant wedding cake.

Over the years it has attracted some endearing quotes. That distinguished architect Sir Edwin Lutyens observed: 'Very naughty, but in the right spirit'. DP Mortlock in *The Popular Guide to Norfolk Churches*, noted po-faced: 'The crocketting (is) so lush it verges on the fungoid'. The unidentified essayist in the Redundant Churches Fund's gazetteer, *Churches in Retirement*, described it as 'riding the cornfields of mid-Norfolk, its crazy towers uninhibited by the solid splendour… of its neighbours **Cawston** and **Salle**'.

Inside it's just about as Mr Elwin left it - and maintains the promise of the exterior: huge operatic oak angels with outspread wings on the **hammerbeams** of the chancel roof, a throne-like pulpit - and a complete scheme of pretty good contemporary stained glass. Though even here, the Rector was, in the words of that vastly knowledgeable expert on Norfolk glass, David J King, 'carried away on flights of iconographical fancy'.

Still, it's fun. Though legend has it that, when Mr Elwin had spent his lifetime and a fortune on his creation, his long-suffering wife complained that she was still waiting for the rectory kitchen to be redecorated!

Now to a very different church, **Bressingham St John**, down in the south of the county near Diss, where the elegant tower draws you to it from afar and its super clerestory brings you to a dazzled halt. The first is 15th century Perpendicular, the second 16th century Tudor, dashingly intermixing contrasting stone and flint. Inside, the focus of interest, after admiring the fine **arch-braced** and **hammer-beamed roof**, is a superb set of bench pews made for the church during its 16th century rebuilding. The bench ends are amazingly opulent in their carving, crowned by **poppyheads**, with animals and birds at the corners, and curious figures and dynamic shapes and patterns. For these alone this splendid church would be worth a visit. There are hosts of excellent bench pews and bench ends in Norfolk, but a particularly fascinating set will be found at **Forncett St Peter**, south-east of Wymondham. This is an especially pretty church, with a gorgeous **Saxon** round tower worth going far to see. There is much of interest inside, but it is the benches which attract the eye, not just as a set but individually, for each one is different.

There is, for example, one that looks like a woman in a sentry box - though it could be **Mother Julian of Norwich**, the 14th century anchoress, that is, a religious recluse who chose to be walled up in her cell, in order to devote her life to prayer and piety. Find the huntsman with his horse and falcon; and the miser with his coin box... and a grinning devil in attendance.

Pews of a very different kind, plain, upright box pews, take us to a particular era of churchmanship; and to a layout of furnishings known as **Prayer Book Churches**. Enough to say here that those furnishings, seemly and simple, were low communion tables, three-decker pulpits and box pews.

Norfolk has especially fine examples at **Bylaugh**, near Dereham; and **Warham St Mary**, just inland from Wells. **Thurning** (between Reepham and Holt), **Gunton** (in the north-east of the county) and **Wilby** (south of Attleborough) also merit a visit.

Wilby All Saints is a fine, spacious church, largely of 14th and 15th century date, and with an interior Prayer Book layout of quiet delight which has hardly changed since 1633, presided over by a very fine three-decker pulpit.

Give yourself time at Wilby, there is so much to see. It also remains firmly in this writer's memory as the church where, through the simple expedient of poking his head into an unexplained recess in the wall, he discovered what may well have been a **wafer oven** - used to bake the wafers for the mass. Only around ten churches in the county still have them.

In his book, *Churches the Victorians Forgot*, Mark Chatfield wrote of **Warham St Mary**: 'This lovely interior, calm and moving, is one of the most memorable in the whole of East Anglia'. Though its three-decker pulpit and high box pews are a late creation, of 1800-1, they are wholly in the spirit of 150 years earlier.

Now to **Bylaugh St Mary the Virgin**. This is a small church tucked away in the countryside (its

North Tuddenham offers a notable painted rood screen, excellent medieval stained glass – and a fine 15th century east window with corbel heads which are a lesson in the clothing styles of the period.

only neighbour is a sewage farm). But what you find inside is an untouched layout from about the same period as that at Warham St Mary… box pews in rich-coloured oak and a superb three-decker pulpit, without doubt the best set in the county.

So peaceful and tranquil it is in St Mary's that the real world seems very far away. A Christmas carol service here, all in candlelight (there is no electricity) is an unforgettable experience, like slipping back in time.

Just a short distance across country from Bylaugh is **North Tuddenham St Mary**, where the accent is on a 15th century screen which is fascinating for its varied gallery of saints; and on some exceptional stained glass.

Saints are numerous indeed in St Mary's. In glass, paint and stone, this writer has counted some forty-five representations of thirty-two of them. It is a handsome church, St Mary's, with its big mid-14th century tower and the rest **Perpendicular** in character. It is one of those many Norfolk churches serving a scattered parish of small population, yet maintained in beautiful order by a devoted small group of people.

Inside, the little screen under the tower, with its late 14th century paintings of Matthew, Mark, Gregory and Augustine, was rescued from a lumber shop. The superlatively painted chancel screen belongs here and requires a detailed guide, for its saintly gathering has some unusual names - like Roche (or Roch, or Rocco), caring saint of plague victims, who is rarely represented in England and twice in Norfolk, here and at Stalham (see him pulling up his robe to reveal the mark of the plague on his left leg).

Then there is Geron (or Gereon or Jeron), again very rare, a nobleman who gave up all to serve God, and seen here as a priest but with a nobleman's falcon on his gloved hand.

The remarkable collection of Norwich School stained glass of the 15th century came here only at the turn of the 1900s - it was discovered, and rescued, by the rector from a builder's yard in Dereham. 'Definitely the chief treasure of the collection', in the words of David King, Norfolk's expert in this field, is a small figure high up on the south side of the nave of St Lawrence, with his

emblem of a gridiron - he shares with St Faith the unhappy significance of having been martyred by being roasted alive upon just such a gridiron. Opposite, in the traceries high in the nave's north wall, are two very curious representations with a fascination of their own. In the easternmost window, find John the Baptist in his rough garb. Look closely (ideally with binoculars) and you'll see an odd serpent-like shape hanging between his knees. As the medieval artist knew, John wore a camel-hair shirt. Logical therefore that he should have a camel's head swinging from it!

In the centre window we find Moses in a wonderful, glowing picture. Glowing too are the strange 'horns' thrusting out from each side of his head. In his definitive book on the subject, *The Norwich School of Glass Painting in the 15th Century*, Christopher Woodforde provides the fascinating explanation. In *Exodus 34, v. 30*, the Bible tells us that when Moses came down from Mount Sinai, the Israelites saw that 'the skin of his face shone; and they were afraid to come nigh him'. Mr Woodforde tells us that the Hebrew verb for 'shone' is also the root of the noun meaning 'horn'. Translated into Latin it became *facies cornuta* - and from as far back as the 11th century, medieval artists interpreted this as saying that Moses had 'shining horns' rather than shining skin. There is a similar horned Moses - but not so good as North Tuddenham's example - in the north aisle of **Norwich Cathedral**.

Before one leaves St Mary's it is worth taking a walk outside round the east end. The chancel east window is very good 15th century Perpendicular - but that too was brought here from elsewhere, again by the Revd. Robert Barry, who installed the glass. To each side of the window are craftsmanly carved corbel heads. In them we have an example of how medieval artists always chose to represent the costumes of their day, rarely those of Christ's epoch - and in so doing gave us a very accurate guideline to the date of their work.

On one side of the window is a portrait head of a gentleman in a soft cap; opposite, his lady sports a frilly headdress. This means we can date them within a ten-year span, about 1450-60, in the reign of Henry VI. It also means we can visualise the rest of their clothes: he would have worn a full-length gown, trimmed with fur and with full sleeves. She a high-waisted gown and long, soft draperies.

It cannot be repeated often enough that church buildings are not dry history and repositories of medieval art. They are living things reflecting the shifts and turns of living history. More, they are about people: the people who built them, the people through the centuries who worshipped there, who lived through changing and unsettling times; yet kept their trust and passed these buildings on to us in faith.

At **Ludham St Catherine** we have a vivid mirror to just such changing and unsettling times, when the lives of church and people were shaken as never before or since.

In the later years of Henry VIII, and more particularly during the kingship of his young and sickly son, Edward VI - a fervent Protestant, despite his tender years - appalling vandalism was done in our English churches in the name of ridding the realm of popery and superstition. Across the chancel arch were placed, immemorially, the rood - a beam bearing the figures of Christ, his mother and St John; below, the rood loft; and at ground level, the screen. Roods were among the first things to be swept away and destroyed as the reforming zeal took hold.

In place of the rood, in many cases, went boards on which were painted the Royal Arms - signifying that the king was supreme governor of the Church of England - together with improving scriptural quotations.

Edward reigned for just six years and died aged sixteen. To the throne then came catholic Mary - who ordered that all be put back in our churches as it was before the break with Rome.

Putting back the rood quickly had its problems. The three figures were traditionally fully carved and about five feet high. Many churchwardens chose a short cut - have a painting of the rood done directly onto the boards, over the top of the Royal Arms, or onto new boarding.

This is probably what happened at Ludham. But then Mary died, after just five years on the throne. And with the accession of Elizabeth I came the command: As you were before Mary - and this time my coat of arms must take centre place in the chancel arch over the screen.

So what did the canny churchwardens of Ludham do? They had Elizabeth's arms painted on canvas - and stretched it across over the rood painting. At some point the canvas was pulled off, and last century was put on the back of the rood painting, looking down onto the altar. And thus you find it now, a record of tempestuous events of 450 years ago.

The Ludham screen, by the way, which came through all this unscathed, is exceptional both in design and carving and in its fine paintings of saints, amongst whom are Apollonia (whom we met at Barton Turf) and Norfolk's own gentle farmer saint, Walston. The son of a prince who chose a life of poverty, he lived out his pious life at Bawburgh, near Norwich, and his death brought miracles as gentle as his character. For centuries, until it was destroyed at the Reformation, his shrine attracted numberless pilgrims.

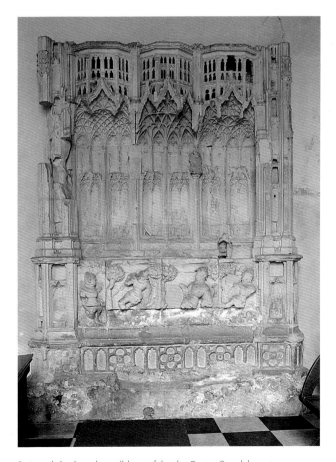

Battered, broken, but still beautiful – the Easter Sepulchre at Northwold, the finest survivor of its kind in the county, recalling the ritual and ceremony of the English Church before the Reformation.

If endearing cults like those of St Walstan, and a general reverence for saints, were part of the religious and everyday life of the Middle Ages, at the very centre of their religious year was the ritual and significance of the **Easter Sepulchre**. These were structures, often temporary, but also permanent, placed in the north wall of the cancel beside the altar. They were the centre of elaborate rituals extending from the Thursday of Holy Week through Good Friday and Easter Saturday, and on to Easter morning.

Most today show us only a recess in the chancel wall, though **Northwold** (in the deep south-west of the county) has a wonderful survivor, carved in chalk, possibly in the late 14th century: despite being cruelly mutilated, it still gives an indication of its former beauty and splendour. There is another at **Kelling**, and a third, small but richly carved, at **Baconsthorpe** (both are near Holt). Apart from these three, hints of at least thirty more exist in Norfolk's churches.

On Maundy Thursday Mass was celebrated with extra solemnity and three Hosts (the bread, the Body of Christ) were consecrated, one for the priest at this Mass, another for Good Friday - and a third which would be 'buried in the tomb' - that is, placed within a pyx (a receptacle, normally suspended over the altar, to contain the reserved sacrament) - together with a crucifix, representing the very cross on which Christ hung.

This happened on Good Friday evening, to the accompaniment of solemn chanting and prayers, when the church was in deepest mourning, all altars stripped, candles extinguished, the high altar curtained off with a **Lenten veil**.

From then onward, sepulchre and 'body' were watched night and day until early on Easter Morning when joyful celebration and chanting took the place of solemnity. All the lights were re-lit. The 'buried' host was removed to the high altar, and the crucifix removed from the sepulchre to be taken in triumphant procession around the church, as the bells rang out and voices were raised in the joyful anthem Christus Resurgens, Christ is Risen. In this ritual and ceremonial, we reach back to the very spirit, the mystery, of the life of the church and its people in the later Middle Ages. To stand before an **Easter Sepulchre** today, be it a plain recess in the wall or the carved echo of former glories like that at Northwold, and to let one's mind reach out, is to touch for a moment the medieval world which the Reformation effectively brought to an end. It also serves to underline, in a profound sense, what a priceless heritage has been handed down to us in our great treasury of Norfolk churches.

PRESERVING OUR HERITAGE

NORFOLK CHURCHES TRUST

Norfolk Churches Trust was set up in 1976 to assist Norfolk's great heritage of churches. Its purpose and role is to keep them open as places of worship through advice and provision of funds. With the generous help of the county and district councils, the annual fund-raising Bicycle Ride and its own fund-raising, some £200,000 each year is allocated in grants. For membership and other information contact the NCT at 9 The Old Church, St Matthews Road, Norwich NR1 1SP.

The Story of the Photographs

After seven years of photographing them I still push open the door of every new church with a thrill of expectation. Each church is so different and so many generations have come and gone and left their stamp upon them. Working alone inside them they cast a spell and it is impossible not to feel the presence of all the souls that have worshipped there, often since Norman and even Saxon times.

When I first got the inspiration to photograph churches I was lucky to have the guidance of Paul Cattermole, a leading local authority, who impressed on me that there was a code to be broken before one could fully appreciate the true marvels of these venerable old buildings. Obviously there was a great deal to learn, but in happy ignorance I took the plunge and, armed with an indispensable Munro Cautley guide book (out of print and thus extremely expensive) I began my daunting task. Quite soon I was totally hooked and now with over six hundred East Anglian churches photographed I am an addict.

Many of my pictures are just interesting records of old buildings but every now and then a touch of magic has crept in, as it so often does when you are photographing something you love. Every photographer will know these moments and I remember most vividly certain special occasions; the yellow light from a winter sun picking out a distant church tower; a flock of sheep peacefully grazing in the foreground of a lonely little church; sunshine on beautiful old benches; a field of Norfolk poppies stretching towards a far away church; the sunlit alabaster effigy of an old knight and his lady in eternal sleep. I use my camera (an old Canon 35mm SLR) as a kind of 'Instant Sketchbook'; its ultra sharp lenses faithfully record the minutest detail as well as spanning great vistas of the East Anglian landscape. I also believe in travelling light and carry the absolute minimum of equipment, relying almost entirely on natural light.

A very rewarding aspect of the work has been our exhibition 'Churches in the East Anglian Landscape' which, with the help of my colleague Mike Fuggle, we have shown all over East Anglia (and even in Europe) and which has been seen by many thousands of people. I plan to leave this large collection of exhibition pictures to Norwich Cathedral where I hope they will eventually be able to enjoy a permanent home. My collection of transparencies is now housed in the Norfolk Library where they will shortly be accessible to the public via their new image database system.

There are around 650 medieval churches in Norfolk (a greater concentration than anywhere else in Europe it is said) and so sadly it has not been possible to include all of them. Some very distinguished churches have had to be left out but my hope is that our selection contains examples from the small and humble as well as the grand and stately and goes some way towards showing the beauty of our great heritage.

Richard Tilbrook April 1997

Ashwellthorpe All Saints

map ref. J8

Ashwellthorpe is the home village of Richard Tilbrook, who has taken all the photographs for this book, so a self-portrait against the backdrop of his own church seemed appropriate. All Saints takes the eye with its high and elegant

Perpendicular nave, 13th century tower and 14th century chancel. Among its numerous details is an ancient, crafted door handle. Apart from being high, the nave is also exceptionally wide inside, and beautifully light. The particular treasure here, as detailed in the introductory text, is the lovely alabaster tomb of 1417 of Sir Edmund Thorp and his wife Joan, of whom fuller details are given in the introduction on page xi.

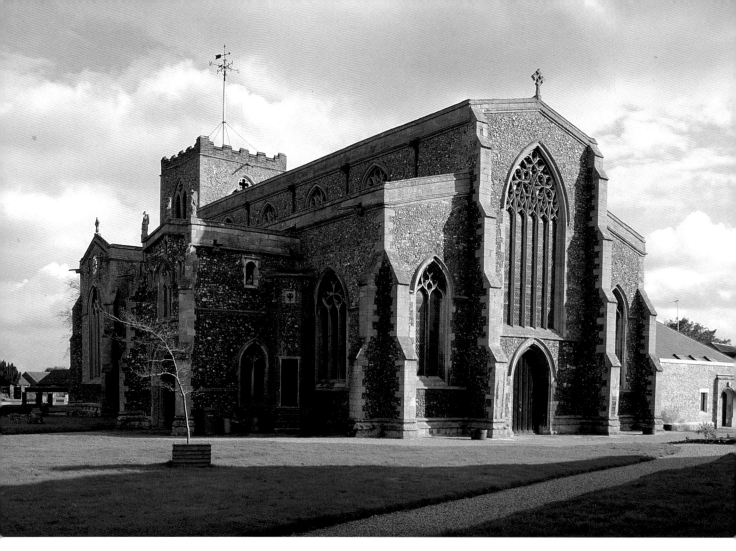

Attleborough
Assumption
of the Blessed
Virgin *map ref.* G8

This is a grand town church which once was even larger – there was once a noble chancel to the east of the tower, which served as a College of Priests, but this was demolished at the **Reformation** when Henry VIII broke with Rome. The massive tower is **Norman** at its base. The rest of the church, including the

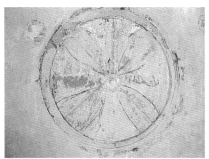

north porch with its vaulted ceiling locked by a carved roof **boss**, is 15th century. Attleborough's great glory is its spectacular **rood screen**, given by a local family in 1475, which against all the odds survived the Reformation and the centuries since. An equally important and rare survivor is the mural

painting of about 1500 above the screen. Its principal subject is the **Annunciation**, when the Archangel Gabriel brought to Mary the news that she would bear the Christ child. To the left, note Attleborough's **scratch dial** – an ancient time-piece explained in the feature panel on page 38.

Bale
All Saints

map ref. G2

All Saints is a most attractive church
in a fitting village setting, not least the
handsome grove of small-leafed oaks
under which one walks into the
churchyard. The church is largely
14th century, though its lovely **chancel**
is from about 1300. There's a very
good **font** of about 1470; an
interesting survivor in the shape of a
pulley-block whose job was to raise
and lower the candle-beam which lit
the **rood** figures below the chancel
arch; and some high quality 15th
century Norwich stained glass
together with some 14th century
work. Although the church is
dedicated to All Saints, there seems
to have been a particular devotion
here to the **Annunciation**, when
Gabriel appeared to Mary to tell her
of the birth of Christ. In the detail
seen here, the Holy Ghost in the form
of a dove comes to the Virgin.

Barton Turf St Michael and All Angels

map ref. M4

In the heart of Norfolk's Broadland is this beautiful building in its rural setting, giving the appearance of all being of a piece from the 15th century. The heart of the church is older, however, late 13th/early 14th century, as seen in the **nave** arcade arches. The special feature here is the 15th century **rood screen** to **chancel** and south aisle. The chancel screen is a wonder, with its rare

representations of the **Nine Orders of Angels**, as detailed in the introductory text to this book on page xii. The aisle screen is distinguished by its paintings of four kings: Edmund king and martyr, Edward the Confessor, Henry VI; and Olaf (or Holofius), king of Norway, with a loaf of bread – a pun on his name, 'whole loaf'.

Beeston-next-Mileham Nativity of the Blessed Virgin

map ref. E5

Back in 1962, Sir Nikolaus **Pevsner** called this 'The best church by far in this strangely obscure and inaccessible area'. Certainly this is a splendid and interesting building. The spire is a 19th century rebuild, but the rest is largely 14th century, with some quite splendid **reticulated** windows – the peak of **Decorated** style achievement which was largely brought to a halt by the Black Death of 1349.

This is an interior to make one stop and catch one's breath in sheer pleasure. It is light, spacious and lofty, and crowned by splendid **hammerbeam** roofs in **nave** and aisles whose untreated old oak adds a special quality to the overall effect. In the nave, wallposts (posts fixed to the wall while supporting the roof structure) carry impressive carved figures. **Parclose** screens enclose chapels in both aisles, but that in the north aisle is especially fine.

Porches and North Doors

A church **porch**, on the face of it, would seem to serve a simple purpose like any other porch – to provide an entrance and to keep wind and rain off the door! But in the late medieval years, they served a variety of purposes. Porches didn't come to be an integral part of churches until the 14th century, but having done so, they became an essential part of parish life. Part of the burial service took place here. In the porch the priest might give absolution (forgiveness) to a kneeling penitent. Part of the wedding service took place here. When in the fullness of time children were born, the first words of their baptismal service would be spoken in the porch – and the mother who bore them would be 'churched' (purified). The porch proved also to be a useful meeting place for carrying out parish and other business. Another of its uses was as one of the 'stations' in the Sunday and Feast Day

processions, complete with processional cross, candles and banners, which were a natural part of medieval worship. This provides a direct link with **North Doors**. The majority of churches have their main entrance on the south side. But there was also a north door which today one often finds has been filled in.

That door too was part of those regular processions, enabling the ceremonial to extend in and out of the building and around it. But time has invested these doors with a delightful legend – that they were built for Satan's convenience. The story went like this: If as parishioners entered the church they dipped their fingers into holy water in the stoup by the door, and crossed themselves, the devil, were he around, was sure to flee. And to make it quicker and easier for him to go, what better than to give him his own door.

This is, by any measure, a highly individual church, created upon the shell of a medieval building in the 19th century by the rector, the Revd Whitwell Elwin. It was finished in 1891, having taken him near 50 years. It is, you might say, gothic fantasy – it is described in the introductory text to this book on page xiv. You might be appalled, or astonished, or delighted. But no-one can be indifferent. No tour of Norfolk's churches is quite complete without a visit to Booton.

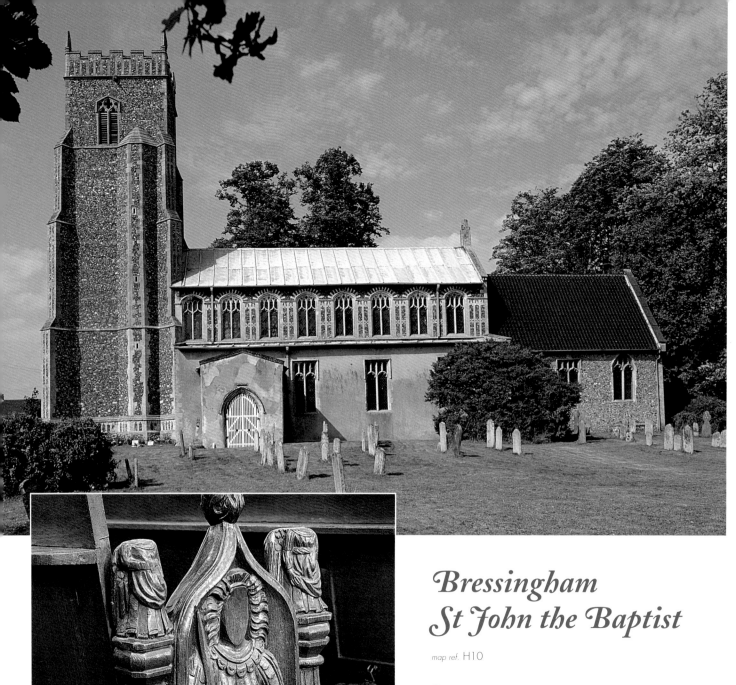

Bressingham
St John the Baptist

map ref. H10

Sir Roger Pilkington rebuilt the body of St John's in 1527, and what a glorious job he made of it. Just look at that eight-window **clerestory**, dashing in its mix of contrasting stone and flint. In his rebuilding, it seems fairly clear that he kept the lower walls of the previous church, for there's a 14th century **sedilia** in the **chancel**. There's a fine **arch-braced** and **hammer-beamed** roof: but what always attracts the visitor is the 15th century set of bench pews, which are amazingly opulent in their bench end carvings, ranging from birds and animals to grotesques.

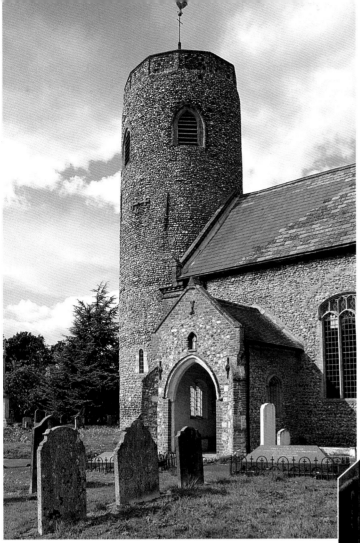

Brooke St Peter

map ref. L7

At least the lower part of the tower is **Norman**, upper windows probably 13th century, as is the south doorway itself, with its superb, heavily traceried door. The body of the church is greatly restored, but still full of interest. Here at Brooke is one of the 37 **Seven Sacrament fonts**, almost all of the 15th century, to be found in Norfolk and Suffolk. These remarkable treasures show on seven panels round the bowl the seven sacraments of the church, and on the eighth, a biblical subject like the Crucifixion, as at Brooke. A memento of a more recent past is the hour-glass stand, complete with **hour glass**, beside the pulpit... a relic of the 17th and 18th centuries, when sermons were very long... and the glass might be turned over 'for the second hour'. Take a close look at the double **piscina** in the sanctuary, rustic and appealing. Easily dated too: double piscinas had only a brief appeal, about 1300 to 1320.

Brisley St Bartholomew map ref. F4

From whichever direction one approaches Brisley, St Bartholomew's superb **Perpendicular** tower is a focal point, four soaring stages thrusting into the sky, topped by battlements and corner pinnacles. Close to, the tower's west end is still more splendid, with its huge, beautifully traceried window and noble doorway brought together under a single arch, which itself is outlined by a deep **dripstone**, above which alternating brick and flint accentuate the shape. The grandeur continues inside, the eye being swept along the clean-lined beauty of the great 15th century **arcade** arches to the dominatingly enormous **chancel** arch (look behind you and the tower arch is equally impressive), and through the lush tracery of the 15th century screen to the great east window. Many points of interest here, but note especially the richly carved canopies of the **sedilia**, complete with miniature carvings of **pelicans** and lions. Why pelicans? They occupied a special place in Christian symbolism, in the guise of the-pelican-in-her-piety. There are several legends, but that which provides a Christian parallel is of the mother bird killing her young in a fit of anger – and on the third day tearing her own breast with her beak and shedding her blood upon the dead young, whereupon they are brought back to life. Thus Christ shed his blood and rose on the third day, that we might live eternally.

Burgh-next-Aylsham
St Mary the Virgin

map ref. K4

In lush countryside hard by the River Bure, St Mary's is a picture postcard church in a setting from which it seems to have grown as naturally as the greenery around it. Walk in, and two very special things await. First, we find here a **Seven Sacrament font**, the subject of whose eighth panel has inspired much expert disagreement. The latest

scholarship suggests it to be the adoration of the
sacrament contained in a **monstrance**. Secondly,
a wonderful **Early English chancel** of about
1220, with tall **lancet** windows (top right),
decorative arcading on the walls, and an
outstanding doorway of the period leading into
a (Victorian) chapel.

Burnham Deepdale St Mary

Right beside the coast road in North Norfolk sits St Mary's, with an Anglo-**Saxon** tower. The rest is of **Early English** origin, though heavily restored. Inside is a wonderful and exceedingly rare treasure from the **Norman** era: a **font**, featuring a group of 12 panels, simply but vigorously carved, representing the seasons and tasks of the rural year.

Fonts and Holy Water Stoups

Second only to mass/communion in the sacraments of the Christian church is baptism, which takes place at the **font**. That is why the font is always found close to the main entrance into the church, symbolising the fact that it is by means of baptism that mankind can enter into the fellowship of Christ's Church.

The main part of the font is the bowl to hold the **holy water**. Preparing the holy water in medieval times involved a complex ritual. Before the Mass on Sundays, salt and water were both exorcised – that is, the devil driven out – by prayers and repeated signs of the cross. Water and salt were then blessed, and the salt strewn across the water in the sign of the cross.

A small amount of water was placed in a **holy water stoup** in the porch, or just inside the church, so that the faithful might dip in their fingers and cross themselves. The rest of the blessed water was in the font, which was fixed with a locked lid for fear of the water being stolen for magical rites. These lids developed into **covers** and canopies which reached artistic heights of decoration and opulence.

Font bowls too were decorated and embellished, and carved with saintly figures and symbols. Here in East Anglia a very distinctive font developed. This is the **Seven Sacrament Font**. Eight sided, it has representations in panels on seven sides of the sacraments or holy ordinances of the Christian Church: Baptism; Mass; Confirmation; Ordination to Holy Orders; Confession/penance; Marriage; and Last Rites (Extreme Unction, the anointing of the dying). In the eighth panel may be The Crucifixion; the Annunciation (when the Archangel Gabriel brought Mary the news that she would bear the Christ Child); or the Assumption (when the Virgin was taken up into Heaven).

Seven Sacrament Font – see Brooke St Peter page 11.

Burnham Norton St Margaret

map ref. D1

Up on a hilltop, with its pure **Norman** tower (save for its parapet) against the sky, and what from a distance look like **Perpendicular nave** and aisles, St Margaret's makes a delightful composition. But all is not as it seems: the interior is quite different from what one expects. Sweetly plain and unadorned, it has round 13th century pillars down one side of the nave, and octagonal 14th century ones on the other. There are two pulpits, one plain 17th century; the other a superb 'wine glass' example with paintings of the **Four Latin Doctors** and the donor in 1450. The massive squat font is Norman. The **Royal Arms** are for George IV.

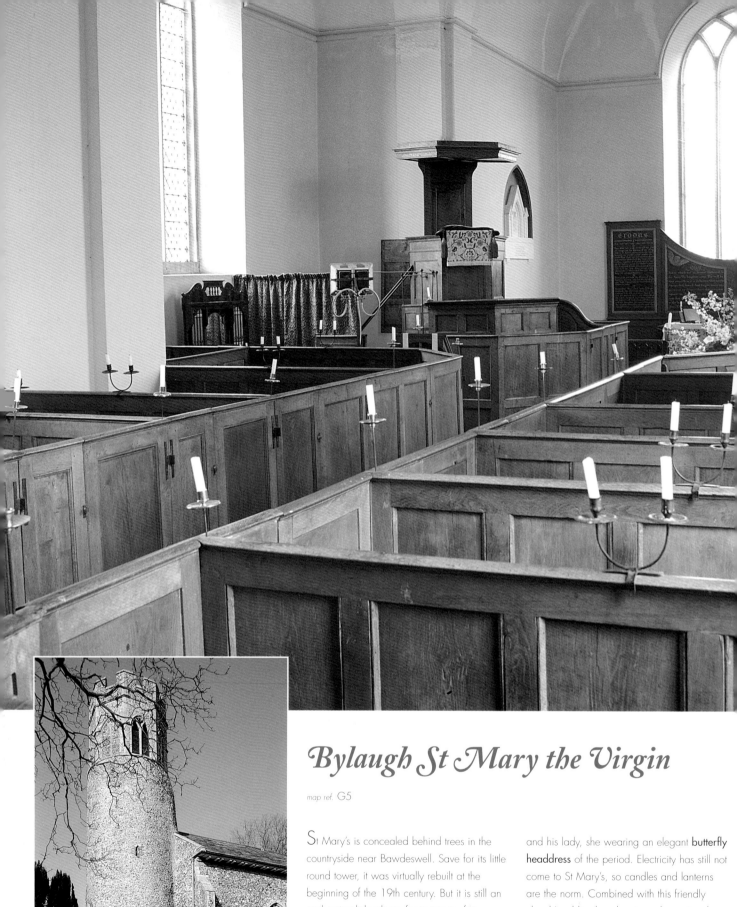

Bylaugh St Mary the Virgin

map ref. G5

St Mary's is concealed behind trees in the countryside near Bawdeswell. Save for its little round tower, it was virtually rebuilt at the beginning of the 19th century. But it is still an enchanting little place, for its interior fittings are lost in a tranquil time warp. Time stopped here in 1809, when its **box pews** and admirable **three-decker pulpit** were installed in the Prayer Book tradition. Don't miss the lovely little memorial brass dated 1471 to Sir John Curson and his lady, she wearing an elegant **butterfly headdress** of the period. Electricity has still not come to St Mary's, so candles and lanterns are the norm. Combined with this friendly church's sublimely calm atmosphere, it makes a candlelit carol service at Christmastime a special experience. Small wonder that the Vicar in Victorian times stayed contentedly here for 74 years, until, in his 90s, he went to his Maker.

Carbrooke St Peter and St Paul

map ref. F7

This is a large and nobly proportioned church with a tall 15th century tower. The rest ranges from the 13th to 15th centuries. Inside, the full view from the tower arch down to the great east window (late 13th century like the **chancel**) is striking, with beautiful, lightly soaring 15th century arcade arches to each side of the **nave**, and enormous **clerestory** windows above. The north aisle altar has a medieval stone **mensa** with five **consecration crosses** and the chancel a lovely 13th century two-seater **sedilia**.

Castle Acre
St James

map ref. D5

St James's, seen from the village street across its immaculately maintained churchyard, is a brave sight, as is described in some detail in the opening text to this book on page viii. Seen from the south side, as in the picture below, it is no less impressive with its great **Tudor** windows with their flattened arches set off by **dripstones** whose shape reminds one of the 'kennel' **headdresses** worn by noble ladies of the Tudor period. Just beyond the tree on the right of the picture is the **priest's door** which once was about 14ft high, possibly to allow a knight to ride into church on his horse to be blessed! St James's superb 'wine glass' **pulpit** of about 1400 is richly painted with figures of the **Four Latin Doctors**. The base of the **rood screen**, which dates from about the same time as the pulpit, has the 12 apostles painted upon it. St Andrew looks as if he's taken a round of lead-shot. Cromwellian target practice perhaps?

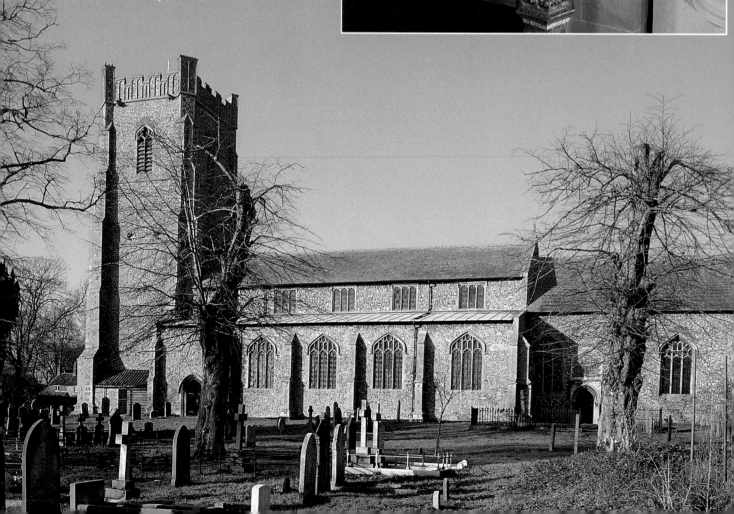

Architectural Styles

1 SAXON TRIANGULAR HEADED

2 SAXON ROUND HEADED

3 Exterior / **4** Interior — NORMAN SLIT

5 Exterior / **6** Interior — EARLY ENGLISH LANCETS

7 SIMPLE GEOMETRIC PLATE TRACERY

8 EARLY ENGLISH LANCETS

9 TYPICAL 'Y' TRACERY OF ABOUT 1300

10 RETICULATED

11 PERPENDICULAR

12 TUDOR

The changing architectural styles in parish churches through a thousand years are best seen and appreciated by the layman in the window designs.

Saxon, 7th century to William the Conqueror's seizure of England in 1066, is notable for its rough construction, for crudely rounded arches and triangular-headed windows and doors (figs 1 and 2, and see Great Dunham and Forncett St Peter, pages 42-3 and 38-9 respectively).

Norman, from the Conquest to about 1200, used small 'arrow slit' windows, usually deeply splayed (figs 3 and 4). Interior architecture displayed massive rounded arches and pillars, and thick walls. Norwich Cathedral is a majestic example; Binham Priory is very fine; and there is a superb arcade at Walsoken. Not to mention the grandeur of the tower at South Lopham (page 86).

Transitional into **Early English**: Transitional was the phase around 1200 when gothic architecture, with its pointed arches, took over from the rounded (Romanesque) arches of the Norman period. Great pillars gave way to slimly elegant, though still rounded ones, and the slim, pointed, Early English **lancet** made its

appearance (figs 5 and 6).

It was not until the second decade of the 13th century that a consistent gothic began to be applied to parish churches. The lancets which had first appeared singly began to be arranged in groups of three (fig 8), five or even seven and the composition to be unified with beautiful containing arch outlines and delicate pencil shafts. From this point onward, builders were seeking to increase space and height and achieve lighter construction, leading to a gradual reduction in the thickness of the walls and still larger areas of window. About half way through the 13th century the lancet began to lose its slim outline and to grow broader as the **Geometric** concept was born. Two lancets together led to the earliest **plate tracery** (fig 7) in which a solid piece of stone was sculpted through to provide a quatrefoil (four leaf) opening, with an element of tracery for the heads of the lancets. From this developed the full Geometric design, in which traceries were made up of separate pieces of stone, making more complex traceries and designs possible. **Bar tracery** had arrived.

From 1300 the **Decorated** period took over, a time of graceful experiment in

flowing and leaping patterns. It began simply enough with the Y-traceried style (fig 9), growing and developing until it reached the full glory of the **reticulated** style (fig 10) taking its name from the Latin *reticulum*, a bag of network. Cley, Beeston-next-Mileham and Great Walsingham, in this volume, have superb examples.

Then in 1349-50 came the disaster of the great plague, the Black Death, when a third of the population of England died and probably half the people of Norfolk, bringing this surge of artistry to an abrupt end.

It was some years before building activity began again. The talent needed to create the full splendour of the Decorated style had largely gone and a simpler way forward was needed. It was the monks of Gloucester who found that way when they invented what we now know as the **Perpendicular** style (fig 11).

Here, the mullions – the uprights in the windows – go straight up to the arch, making it easier to create traceries by working in sections. This style was to prevail for about 250 years, adapted only in its final century by the flattening of the arch to provide the **Tudor** contribution (fig 12).

Cawston
St Agnes

map ref. H4

Michael de la Pole, of the powerful family who were for long Earls of Suffolk, largely rebuilt this magnificent church and its mighty tower in the early 15th century, though he left intact the **chancel** of around 1300. Before going inside, take a look at the vast west window of the tower and the splendid doorway below it, brought together in a fine architectural composition. Look closer at the door: in the spandrels (the angles to each side of the arch) are a wild man with a club, and a dragon. Step into the church, and the prospect is breathtaking, in particular the majestic **hammerbeam** roof of the nave (see next page). Sir Nikolaus **Pevsner**, rarely one to show enthusiasm, proclaimed: 'It is one of the most wonderful in Norfolk... as richly appointed as any'. It has a profusion of angels, tracery, great flowers and **bosses**; and three further figures who may well have stood originally on the **rood** above the chancel screen, though there is not

general agreement about this. The remarkably tall early 16th century screen is painted with no less than 20 saints, including the rarely portrayed Sir John Schorne, who in fact was never actually made a saint, but was honoured for his piety and working of miracles. By all accounts he was a Rector in Buckinghamshire at the beginning of the 15th century. His outstanding achievement was to hoodwink Satan into a boot, where he kept him prisoner. Thus you see Sir John at Cawston carrying the boot, from which a very cross little devil peers out. In the chancel is a remarkable **piscina** carved with a huge dragon and another wild man.

Cley St Margaret

map ref. G1

Stand at the churchyard gate and look up to St Margaret's and you have one of the most glorious sights in Norfolk, a church of splendour, artistry and immense interest. Walk first up to the south porch, a thing of beauty and elegance, built in the early 15th century with an upper chamber lit by two handsome windows and a rich figure

niche between them. Move round to the west front, and there is the immensely impressive six-**light** west window, looking across a peaceful grassy valley to Wiveton church on the opposite rise. Hard to imagine, but when that window was built, this valley was a busy port, jostling with shipping, and bringing to Cley the wealth which

made this church possible. Back now to look again at the south aspect. Fine **Perpendicular** windows to south aisle, and above them, a most unusual and striking **clerestory** of the **Decorated** period – cinquefoil (five leafed) tracery, enclosed in circles, alternating with two light windows. Then we come to the ruined south transept, whose

window tracery miraculously remains intact, for it is a stunningly beautiful example of the **reticulated** style, at the very highest peak of achievement of the Decorated period.

Inside, St Margaret's is full of delights and wonders, brilliantly light and spacious, with great Decorated **arcade** arches to each side of the very

wide **nave**. Both in nave and south aisle, there are carvings in the angles of the arches which indicate a craftsman of joyous humour and liberty of expression – among them an imp with a glass eye; St George, looking less than enthusiastic, fighting a furious dragon; an adorable lion gnawing a bone – and an impish little man

baring his bottom! There are some curious bench-end carvings; a battered **seven sacrament font**, and much, much more besides.

East Harling
St Peter and St Paul

map ref. F9

Though many of the windows are **Perpendicular**, this superb church is largely of 14th century date. The pretty spirelet on the tower – said to have been the pattern for the one on St Peter Mancroft tower in Norwich – dates from the 15th century. It was at that time that a patroness of wealth and

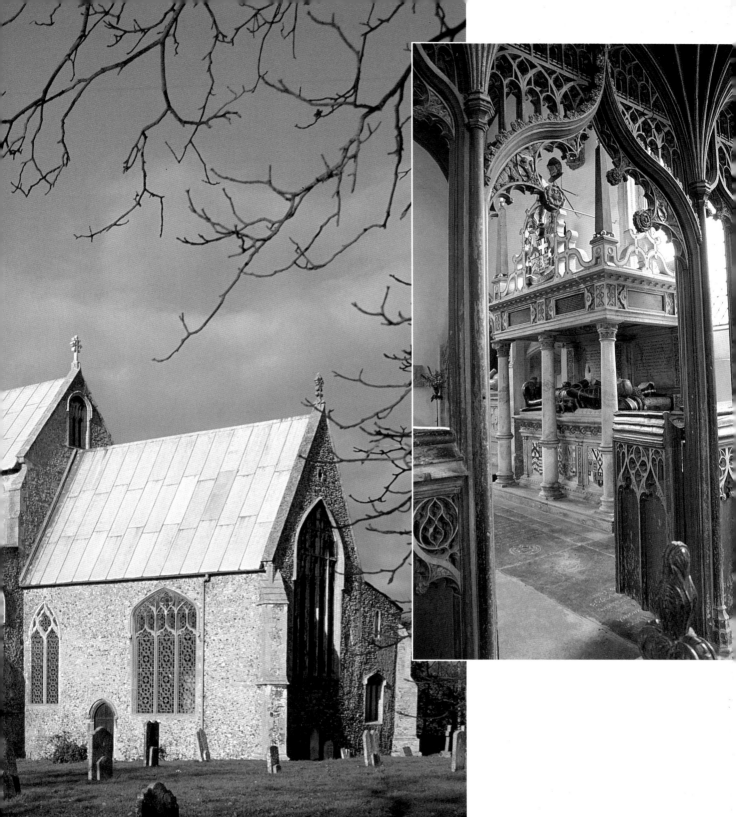

rank, Anne Harling, who died in 1498, set about considerable alterations to the building. She was also responsible, with her second husband Sir Robert Wingfield, for the glass of the famous east window here. Its wonderful workmanship shows no less than 20 scenes, including a superlative

portrait of Sir Robert in tabard (a short cape-like garment worn over the armour and emblazoned with the wearer's coat of arms). The detail pictured overleaf shows the Deposition, the taking down of Christ's body from the cross. There are several magnificent tombs, including that of Sir Thomas

Lovell, 1604 (pictured on previous page); Anne's father Sir Robert Harling, d. 1435; and that of Anne's first husband, Sir William Chamberlain, d. 1462. When Anne died 36 years later her will instructed that she be 'buryed in the chapel of Seint Anne, joyned to the chauncell of the church of the holy Appostellys Seint Peter and Paul in Estharlyng, in the tomb wt my late worshipfull husbond, Sir William Chamberleyn, according to my promyse made unto hym afore this tyme'.

East Tuddenham All Saints

map ref. H6

All Saints sits comfortably in a dip below its village. It is approached through a handsome avenue of lime trees, bringing us directly to the rather fine **Perpendicular porch**. Look closely at the carving in the angles to each side of the outer arch, which combine in an **Annunciation** scene, when Gabriel brought the news to Mary that she would bear Christ. On one side he's doing just that – and enthusiastically waving a banner. On the other Mary is seen with a vase and lily –

emblems of virginity and purity – and the Holy Spirit in the form of a Dove coming down to her in a blaze of sunshine. The inner doorway of the porch is the oldest part of the church, 13th century, as is the sturdy **font**, with rope moulding round the lip and bold scroll foliage round the bowl. Notice how very wide the nave is – 34ft. And don't miss the late 13th century stone effigy of a knight... who in his hands holds his own heart.

Edingthorpe
All Saints

map ref. L2

This is one of those intimate rural churches which, once encountered, is never forgotten. It is set up on a little hill, approached by track – a double bank, in fact, which indicates a defensive position when the lower part of the round tower was built some time between 900 and 1050. The **lych-gate** has a poignant story: it was erected by the rector of the time in memory of his son, who went down with HMS *Royal Edward* when it was torpedoed in the Mediterranean.

From outside, All Saints is a pretty picture of varied window designs of the **Decorated** period. We go in through a simple 12th century doorway, pushing open a door which itself is possibly 14th century.

Inside, all is neatly white washed – skirting some remnants of ancient wall paintings, including a very good St Christopher, discovered under plaster in the 1930s; and a **Seven Acts of Mercy** represented as the branches of a tree. Over the central arch of the beautiful 14th century **rood screen** are two exquisite carved wheel designs; and on its panels, six painted saints with their symbols. Local legend has it that the tiny holes puncturing the lower screen are Roundhead bullet holes: a romantic thought for this most romantic of small churches. Over the old **rood stair** is a notable carved and painted figure niche, contrasting with the simple 17th century **pulpit**.

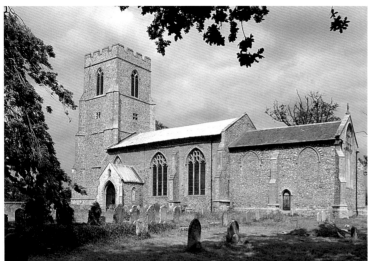

Felbrigg
St Margaret map ref. J2

St Margaret's stands in the park across from 'the big house' (home of the Windhams and their descendants for 350 years until it was handed over to the National Trust by the last of the line). This is a splendid church, beautifully set against mature trees. Inside the big 15th century tower is a small fireplace, which probably served as **wafer oven** (to make the communion wafers for the Mass). The church is handsomely furnished with **box pews**; and **hatchments** decorate the walls. The chief glory here is St Margaret's wealth of fine memorial **brasses** and **monuments**. The great brass to Sir Simon de Felbrygge (died 1351) and his wife is of national importance, not only in its impressive size and outstanding workmanship, but because it is one of only five ancient brasses existing to Knights of the Garter – note the Garter buckled below Sir Simon's left knee. He wears full plate armour, a style in brasses which prevailed from about 1400 (Henry IV) up to the Wars of the Roses in 1455. His lady wears loose flowing drapery and a little dog plays on the hem of her skirts. He was standard bearer to Richard II and she the cousin of Richard's Queen, Anne of Bohemia, whom she served as Maid of Honour.

Tombs and Brasses

Monumental **brasses**, incised with the figures of those they commemorate, are an important feature of many churches. Their value is that they provide 'a commentary on the history, manners and customs of our ancestors' from the end of the 13th to the middle of the 17th centuries.

Of course they pictured the upper crust – nobles, knights, bishops. But it is as memorials of middle class and commonplace life that they are important to us – yeomen, merchants, servants, parish priests, monks, students, people who had no special place in history. But the brass has given them a kind of immortality. What's more, it has given us a complete pictorial history of armour, dress and priestly vestments through 400 years. Brasses are made, by the way, of a remarkably durable alloy of copper and zinc called laton, which was almost all made in Cologne and exported in sheets throughout Europe.

Stone and alabaster tombs, of the grandeur of those seen in these pages at Ashwellthorpe and East Harling, for example, were definitely for the noble born and the very rich, and give us a potent glimpse of the ruling classes of those distant times.

Aumbreys and Chests

Every church had an **aumbrey** – in effect, a simple cupboard, usually in the form of a rectangular recess set into the north wall to the left of the altar at the east end of the church; though it could occasionally be found to the right of the altar, or near to the font at the west end. Aumbries were fitted with secure door and lock, for their purpose was an important one. Their first function was to hold the sacred vessels for the Mass. Sometimes they held also the Reserved Sacrament – that is, the consecrated bread 'reserved' from a celebration of the Mass.

Where there was no **Parish Chest**, they might also be used as a safe for valuables, not only belonging to priest and church but to parishioners.

Very few original aumbries remain intact, though at Great Walsingham there is a rare survival. There are numerous ancient parish chests, massive and substantial, often with three locks whose keys were held respectively by priest and two churchwardens.

Altars and Consecration Crosses

Altars have always been the focal points of Christian churches as the setting for the sacrifice of the Mass. We go back to Roman times for their origins, when early Christians are thought to have celebrated the Mass or Eucharist at domestic wooden tables.

But in the 5th century AD a practice began of celebrating the Mass upon the stone tombs of Christian martyrs, which led in the following century to the general use of stone altars. From then on this became the practice throughout Christendom and remained so in England until the Reformation under Edward VI.

These stone altars were called **mensa** (Latin, table). They carried upon them five crosses, one at each corner and one in the centre, representing The Five Wounds of Christ. These are the wounds He received at the Crucifixion, the nails in hands and feet and the spear thrust in His side.

At the English Reformation in the 16th century, when all images and 'signs of superstition' were declared 'popish' and banned from our churches, the mensa altars were torn down to be replaced by wooden tables. There was often pressure by the authorities that these sacred things should be used in 'profane' ways in order to debase their former sacredness. Thus mensas might be laid down as door steps or pavements in the church.

Similar crosses to those on the altar slabs were also painted or carved upon the walls of churches when the building was consecrated by the Bishop. Three **consecration crosses** were marked in holy oil upon each of the four walls of the church by the Bishop, both inside and out. They were normally at a sufficient height above the ground so that they would not be accidentally brushed by passers by. So during the consecration ceremony, a small ladder was ceremonially carried round so that the Bishop might ascend it to apply the holy oil.

Here in Norfolk the process of removing the stone altars was complete by around 1550. In that year the new Bishop of Norwich, Thomas Thirlby, was installed, and he wrote to his archdeacons to tell them he was aware that 'the mooste parte of all alters within this my diocese be all redye taken downe by commandment of mylorde of Canterbury'.

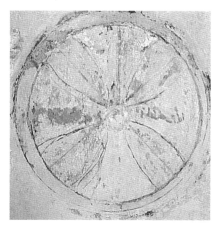

Consecration Cross – see Attleborough St Mary, page 4.

Scratch Dials

On the south walls of some churches, where they may catch the sun, are carved small circles, with a central hole from which radiate lines in varying numbers. These are **Scratch Dials**. In the hole was placed a peg called a *gnomon* (Greek for indicator) which threw a shadow. When it reached one of the lines, it indicated that it was time for an office (a service) or Mass, which explains why this device is also known as a **Mass Dial**. How far back scratch dials go on our English churches is uncertain, but it is likely they were carved through a period spanning the 10th to 14th centuries.

Porches did not become the norm until the 14th century, which explains why some scratch dials will be found inside the porch, out of reach of the sun. They were carved before the porch was built.

Judging the hour by this primitive method goes back far into antiquity. Indeed, we may find in the Bible, in the *Book of Kings* (710 BC) that God 'brought the shadow ten degrees backward, by which it had gone down on the dial of Ahaz'.

Roods and Rood Screens

In medieval times all churches were separated into two – the **chancel**, where the high altar was sited and Mass took place, was the preserve of the priest (thus the separate entrance into chancels – the **priest's door**). The **nave** belonged to the people. Marking this separation was the **rood screen**, with **rood loft** and **rood** above it, an arrangement which every church, even the smallest of them, would have had by the 15th century. The screen explains itself: usually a beautiful, carved and painted work of art, adorned with the painted figures of saints. Above it was a narrow platform, the loft, on or above which was The Rood – figures of Christ at the centre, His mother Mary to the right, and St John the Divine to the left. The loft was approached by rood stairs, set into the wall, many examples of which survive today.

Throughout the week candles were lit upon the loft to light the rood, for which in medieval times there was a great reverence. There is the possibility that on high days and holidays it was used by choristers, and by the priest for the saying of Mass on the Feast of the Holy Cross. But this remains matter for debate.

At the **Reformation** roods and rood lofts were universally torn down and destroyed in the name of ridding England of 'popery', but Attleborough (see page 4) has a gloriously complete screen and rood, which is among the finest survivors in the kingdom.

We have many fine screens in the county. A few churches still have the beam in place which carried the rood loft. Still others have the stone corbels on which the beam rested.

After the excesses during the short reign of Henry VIII's son Edward VI, Elizabeth I restored order, and commanded that, though roods and lofts were unacceptable, every church must have a screen: and that meant putting in a new one if the old one had been destroyed.

Where the rood had been, under the chancel arch, she further commanded that her **Royal Arms** should be set up. More on that in the feature panel on page 92.

Forncett St Peter *map ref.* J8

A picture postcard church, set quietly beyond its village. Its **Saxon** tower is a particular attraction, with its 'portholes' and belfry openings providing copybook examples of simple Saxon style. A very good 15th century **archbraced** roof graces the interior of the church. Note the unadorned Saxon arch into the tower, and how it illustrates just how thick are the tower walls. Below the arch, set into the floor as a step, is an ancient stone altar or **mensa** slab on which two of its five **consecration crosses** can be made out. St Peter's carved bench ends are fascinating – including the curious 'sentry box' pictured here, which just might be **Mother Julian of Norwich** in her **anchorite's** cell.

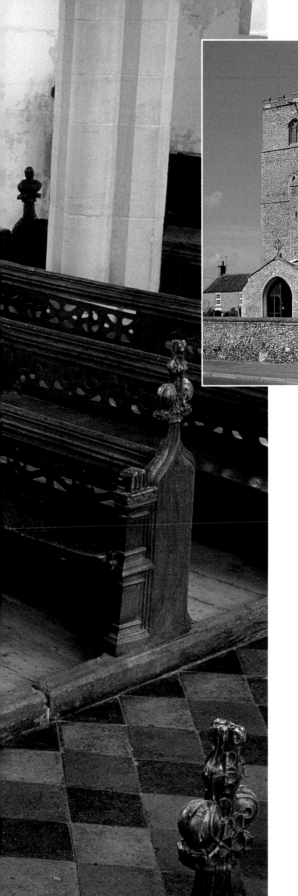

Gooderstone St George

map ref. C7

Assorted architectural styles and outlines lend instant attraction to St George's, which is set off by its powerful tower, whose origins are very likely **Norman** but which now shows an impressive 14th century face, with its excellent west window of the **Decorated** period. **Nave** and **clerestory** are **Perpendicular**, but the **chancel** is **Early English**, of the 13th century. The 14th century porch has a lovely and unusual detail, as pictured here: small round windows with trefoil (three leaf) traceries. The interior is impressive, with attention focussing at once on the complete set of beautiful 15th century benches – rough timbers smoothed by half a millenium of use, and made striking by the pierced-through carving in the backs.

The south aisle has a lushly carved and decorated **piscina** complete with **credence shelf** which before the **Reformation** served a **guild chapel**. Not only striking, but very important, is the unusually tall 15th century **rood screen**: it is remarkable in that it has a very rare survival, a complete bracket, springing outwards from the screen, and the knub-ends of several others. These almost certainly carried statuettes, immediately under the **rood loft**. The chancel east window is a lovely Early English composition (compare with Castle Acre and Little Snoring in the introductory text).

Great Dunham
St Andrew

map ref. E5

In a county so rich in fine medieval churches, there is inevitably a select list which any visitor is urged not to miss. St Andrew's is one of them. Here is not only a fine square **Saxon** tower, set between **nave** and **chancel**, but an interior which breathes the very spirit of a thousand years ago. Sir Nikolaus **Pevsner** was convinced that it is post-Conquest but in Saxon style, but general opinion favours 'Saxon-proper'. The tower's bell openings

are solidly and resoundingly of that period, as are the 'porthole' round openings. In the west base of the tower is a triangular doorway (detail), long since blocked, which again fits unequivocally into the Saxon mould. The window above it, with its interlacing tracery, was put in around 1300. **Perpendicular** windows may have been cut into the little nave. But the interior remains sublimely and simply Saxon, with round-headed **blind**

arcading to each side, and the uncluttered beauty of the nave and chancel arches under the tower. In the serene little chancel is a most attractive 15th century **piscina** with tiny birds delightfully carved in the **spandrels**.

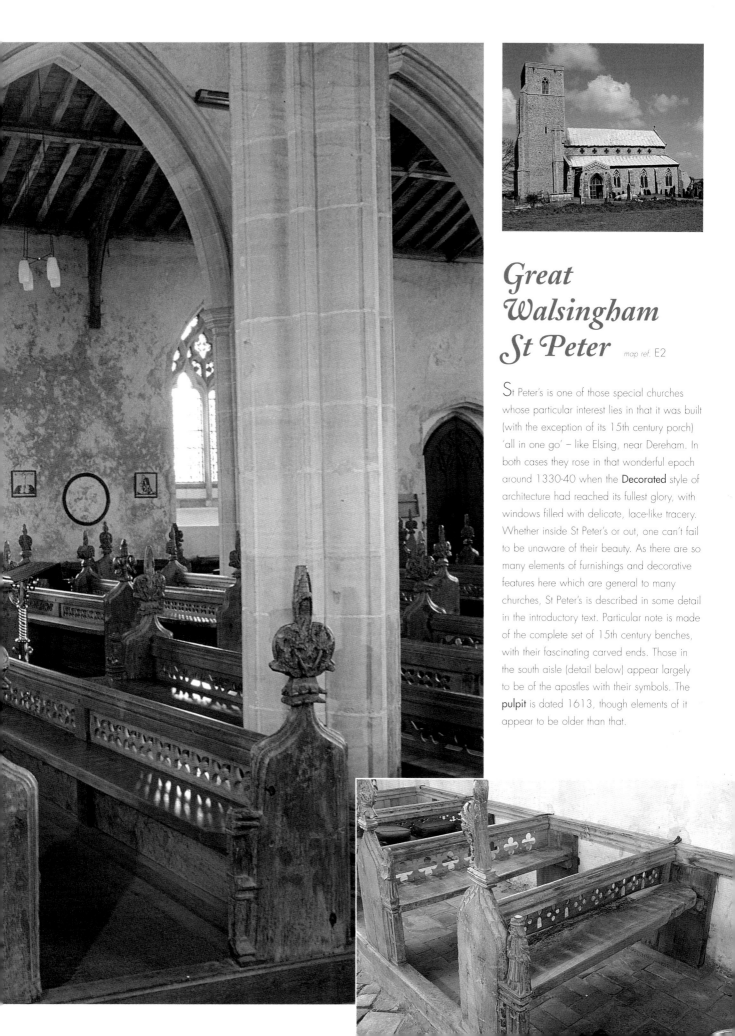

Great Walsingham St Peter *map ref.* E2

St Peter's is one of those special churches whose particular interest lies in that it was built (with the exception of its 15th century porch) 'all in one go' – like Elsing, near Dereham. In both cases they rose in that wonderful epoch around 1330-40 when the **Decorated** style of architecture had reached its fullest glory, with windows filled with delicate, lace-like tracery. Whether inside St Peter's or out, one can't fail to be unaware of their beauty. As there are so many elements of furnishings and decorative features here which are general to many churches, St Peter's is described in some detail in the introductory text. Particular note is made of the complete set of 15th century benches, with their fascinating carved ends. Those in the south aisle (detail below) appear largely to be of the apostles with their symbols. The **pulpit** is dated 1613, though elements of it appear to be older than that.

Great Witchingham
Assumption of the Blessed Virgin

map ref. H4

It looks good with its trim 14th century tower, that fine **clerestory** (look closely: one window is a dummy!), generously adorned **porch** and handsome **aisle** and **transept** windows. Inside, a good **archbraced** roof with a panelled **canopy of honour** at the east end. The impressive eagle lectern is richly carved.

The **seven sacrament font**, which still has a remarkable amount of its medieval colouring, has as its eighth panel the **Assumption** of the Virgin (her translation into heaven).

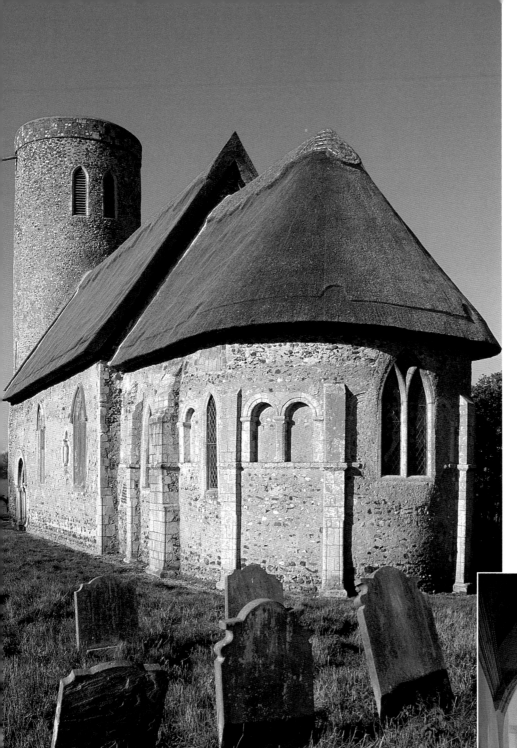

This is an exquisite little church which has remained largely unaltered for 900 years – the small gothic east window dates from about 1300. There is **Norman** arcading round the apse (rounded east end). The entrance door is a wonderful kaleidoscope of Norman decorative devices – wheels, zigzags and bobbings (little cylinders). Carved on the walls are no less than six **scratch dials**. Inside there is a beautiful 15th century **font**, which the doorway frames; beyond it, a **St Christopher** wall painting; other murals also; and the remains of a 15th century screen.

Haddiscoe
St Mary

map ref. M8

On a splendid site and characterised by its wonderfully distinctive tower sits St Mary's. The tower is probably late **Saxon**, just before the Conquest, though its jaunty chequerwork battlements came later, in the 15th century. From the same period comes the **porch**, with its original roof, sheltering a fine 12th century **Norman** doorway carved with zigzags and scallops (cones) and a rather special door which has been described as 'covered with splendidly barbaric ironwork of an early date'. Above the doorway is a very rare Norman sculpture, showing a seated priest, robed in a chasuble (circular or oval garment, with central head opening) and hand raised in blessing. There are **wall painting** fragments, including a **St Christopher** (of about 1400) and traces of a **Three Living and Three Dead** sequence. **Double piscinas** are uncommon: there's a nice one in the 13th century **chancel**.

Harpley
St Lawrence

map ref. C3

A beautiful church in a wooded setting. For 36 years, from 1294 to 1332, John de Gourney was both patron and rector here and he did much rebuilding and alteration. A century after him came more changes, when the Knollys family (pronounce it 'noles' – they are still around) put their **Perpendicular** stamp on the church. The little battlements around de Gourney's south **aisle** are part of the Knollys work: on them you can spot the gridiron emblem of the church's patron saint,

St Lawrence. He shares with St Faith, poor man, the distinction of having been martyred by being burned on such a gridiron. The south **porch** (a Knollys addition) shelters a fine contemporary door with a small wicket set into it. On this are the signs of St Luke (winged ox) and St John (eagle). The interior has masses of interest. The 15th century **archbraced** roof has angels along both **wall plates** and ridge. In both south aisle and **chancel** there are **double piscinas** (see photo

detail), which enjoyed a brief span of popularity at the turn of the 1300s, so we can date them accurately. There's an **Easter Sepulchre** and a great west window packed with ancient glass and a diverse selection of saints, plus members of the **Nine Orders of Angels** – refer to Barton Turf St Michael in the introductory text on page xii.

Heckingham
St Gregory

map ref. M6

A solidly **Norman** church, despite the many window inserts and alterations through the centuries, with its original apsidal (rounded) east end. The round base of the tower is Norman, though the rest of it, in octagonal shape, is difficult to date. The chief glory of this intimate and inviting little place is the spectacular Norman south doorway, one of the best of its kind in England. Notice the different decorations round the arch – wheels, zigzags, bobbins (little cylinders) and wedges, all serving to frame the chunky Norman font on its four squat little legs.

Hemblington All Saints *map ref. M6*

All Saints is a sublimely peaceful little church, with no near neighbours, and a wonderful atmosphere – which might have something to do with the gently overwhelming presence of **St Christopher**, protective patron of travellers. The round tower is **Norman**, though when its odd little cap appeared is problematical. **Nave** and **chancel** look early 14th century. The simple 'hall' interior (nave and chancel are continuous, with no arch between) is charming in its simplicity – yet given a real touch of drama by the immense ancient **wall painting** (discovered under plaster in 1937) of St Christopher wading through a busy river with the Christ-child on his shoulder. A lot of the accompanying scenes

around him showing his life and martyrdom have gone, but several survive.

The **font** here is a beauty. It has seated, carved figures (seven saints and the Holy Trinity) in each of the eight panels round the bowl; and eight standing figures round the base, including six identifiable saints. Spot the one with manacles: that is St Leonard, a nobleman turned monk who in 5th century France served the celebrated King Clovis of the Franks, doughty defender of Christianity. Clovis gave him the right to release any prisoner whom he visited: thus the manacles, and the fact that he's patron saint of prisoners.

Horsham
St Faith
St Andrew

map ref. K5

A large and impressive church, said to have been built by the monks of nearby Horsham Priory, whose interesting remains are now part of a farmhouse. The east end's **Early English** (13th century) **lancet** windows are still intact; the tower is 14th century **Decorated**; the rest **Perpendicular**. The interior is spacious and impressive, with grand 15th century **font** with a handsome **Jacobean**

(17th century) cover. The **pulpit** is rather fine, dated 1480, and is painted with figures of St Faith and St Wandregesilius (he was abbot of Fontanelle in the 7th century: the church at Bixley, south of Norwich, is the only one in all England dedicated to him). The screen was given by wealthy parishioners in 1528. It has 12 paintings of saints but two are very unusual – St Bridget

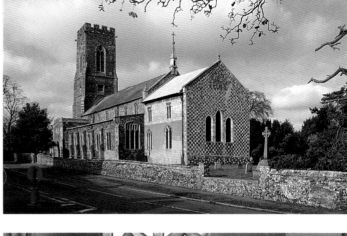

(or Birgitta) of Sweden, seen receiving revelations from God; and St Catherine of Sienna, both 14th century mystics whose writings had a profound influence in their day on the spiritual lives of men and women involved in everyday affairs. Why they are here at Horsham is matter for conjecture.

King's Lynn
St Margaret

map ref. A4

St Margaret's is the mighty town church of an ancient borough. **Norman** originally, largely rebuilt in the 13th century – when its present length of 235 feet was set down – and much altered through the centuries, it needs a whole day and copious description to appreciate all its detail. Enough here to point out a few of its gems: worthy of close attention is the opulent and richly carved Georgian **pulpit**; the beautiful 15th century **clerestory** with a gallery walk; two of the largest and most splendid memorial **brasses** in England, both of the mid-14th century; a set of finely carved **misericordes** of about 1370, including a very sinister **Green Man** swathed in oak leaves; and a lovely 13th century **chancel**.

Church Roofs

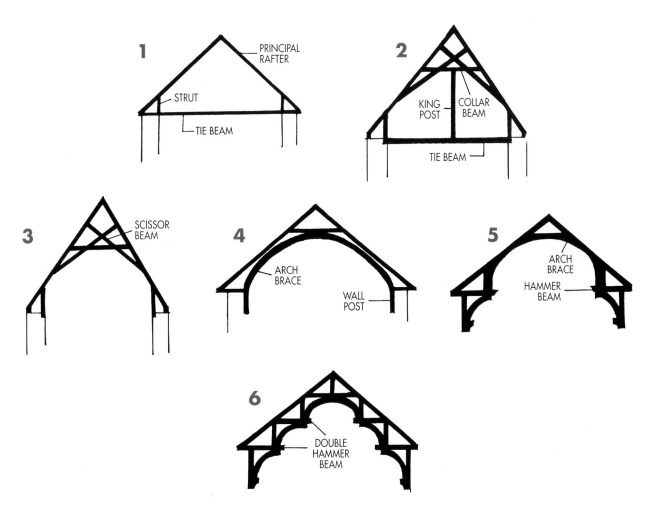

1 — PRINCIPAL RAFTER, STRUT, TIE BEAM

2 — KING POST, COLLAR BEAM, TIE BEAM

3 — SCISSOR BEAM

4 — ARCH BRACE, WALL POST

5 — ARCH BRACE, HAMMER BEAM

6 — DOUBLE HAMMER BEAM

Church **roofs** and their construction are a considerable subject on their own.

The simplest form is a series of rafters held firmly, for strength, by a **tie beam** across the full width of the space below (fig 1), with its two ends fixed to **wall plates** (timbers laid along the length of the top of the wall).

Sometimes there is a vertical post rising from the tie beam to support the roof at a higher point. This is called a **king post** (fig 2), which rises to meet a **collar beam**.

Another system is the **scissor beam** (fig 3), which can exist with its own crossed beams alone, or with a collar. This arrangement had the advantage of not intruding on the space below, and giving an impression of greater openness.

A cleaner line was provided by **archbraces** – solid pieces of timber in arch form, rising up the line of the roof (fig 4). To insure against the possibility of the roof spreading outwards, the arch was continued down to wall posts, through which the wall itself acted as a brace against spreading.

It was the use of **wall posts** which made possible the magnificent development of the **hammerbeam** (fig 5). Basically this is arched braces cantilevered (projecting outwards) on horizontal beams, which in turn are supported by smaller arched braces fixed to the wall posts. From there it was a natural development to the **double hammerbeam** (fig 6).

In both hammers and double hammers, the medieval carpenters and artists took the opportunity to add carved angels and other rich decorations, resulting in memorable roofs such as those at Cawston, Knapton, Necton, South Creake (all featured in this volume) and others in the county.

Knapton St Peter and St Paul

map ref. L2

A good looking church set high above the village street. Note that the **priest's door** into the **chancel** has its own little **porch** over it – a local feature this: there's another, even more interesting, at nearby Trunch. But one comes here for two things in particular – the **nave** roof, and the **font**. The roof, datable to 1504, is one of the best in the county, a carpenter's masterpiece, **double hammerbeam** in style, enormous in its proportions – and with squadrons of angels, 138 in all. The font is octagonal, 13th century and unusual, standing on stumpy legs and raised up on three steps. Its cover is quite modern in contrast, 1704. But it's a delight, cheerfully coloured, shaped like a bandstand in the park. Round it is painted a Greek inscription which translates jauntily; 'Wash my sins and not my face only'. It also happens to be a palindrome – that is, it reads the same backwards or forwards.

Little Snoring St Andrew

map ref. F2

A delight of a church which is described in some detail in the opening text to this book, since in its small span it contains an astonishing range of architectural styles, as well as much else to interest the curious visitor. Here we see how the church is offset from its tower, which served an earlier church whose western outline is still evident. The pretty **porch** of about 1300 shelters a truly eccentric bit of workmanship – a re-used **Norman** door which has been knocked, possibly with more vigour than artistry, into a pointed, gothic arch shape. The interior is all simplicity and peace. The sturdy **font**, boldly carved with foliage, is Norman.

Loddon
The Holy
Trinity

map ref. M7

There were two churches on this site before the present one. Then in 1486 a great local magnate started again, so all is in the full burgeoning of **Perpendicular**. One of its splendours must have been its **seven sacrament font**, set on its elaborately carved, stepped platform. Then in the 1640s came Civil War and the **Puritan** mission to destroy imagery and popery. The town book of 1642 tells

all: the sum of six shillings was 'laide out to Rochester, the glaser, defasinge of the Images in the Church'. He did a thorough job: not one detail of the eight carved panels around the font remains. The 15th century **rood screen** is painted with scenes, including (see detail) the killing of **St William of Norwich** – a shameful myth passed down as history.

Ludham St Catherine

map ref. M5

A grand church, sitting in its big, well-tended churchyard, and surrounded by attractive old village houses. The big, straightforward tower is 14th century; the neat 15th century **porch** protects a plain 13th century doorway. The **clerestory** is 15th century too, as are the tall **arcade** arches

As the opening text to this book explains, this painted rood scene at Ludham was hurriedly done when Mary ascended the throne in the wake of Edward VI's destruction of rood figures and lofts. Then came Elizabeth I, who ordered that her coat of arms be put up in all chancels in this position. So at Ludham the arms were painted on canvas, and stretched over the rood scene. Much later the canvas was removed, lost for a while – then put on the back of the rood painting, looking down onto the altar, where it remains now.

below it. It is a fine prospect as you enter the church and look down its whole length to the great five-light east window with its superb **reticulated** tracery. The **nave** roof is **hammerbeam** and **archbraced**, and in the spandrels, the triangular shapes between hammerbeams and

roof, one can make out the wheel emblem of the church's patron saint. It is the **chancel** arch however on which attention focuses here. Firstly for the **tympanum** – the fitting within the arch itself – which is pictured and explained top right, and also in the concluding part of the opening text of

this book. Secondly for the admirable **rood screen**, undoubtedly one of the best in Norfolk, for its superb carving and its 12 very good painted saints, among them Apollonia (see Barton Turf) and Walstan, Norfolk's farmer-saint.

Merton
St Peter

map ref. E8

Just within the park which has been the domain of the de Grey family for many centuries is St Peter's, which sits tranquilly among trees, and is a surprise package of interest and detail. The tower, both in its belfry openings and its solid, totally plain arch into the nave inside the church, suggest **Saxon**. But though the tower base is pre-Conquest, the rest is **Norman**. The body of the church is almost wholly of around 1300 and a little later – walk round the outside and its windows are quite fascinating. Not least is this so in the **chancel** north wall, as can be seen clearly in this photograph: the tracery shapes are **Decorated** in influence, but the construction method harks back more than a century to **plate tracery** when the shapes were knocked through solid stone. Facing the entrance door is a six-sided **font**, unusual in this locality, which has been badly battered through the years. Across in the corner of the south **aisle**, plain **Jacobean** panelling encloses a family pew for the de Greys. The **piscina** and the large **squint**, giving a view of the high **altar**, indicate a pre-**Reformation** chapel here. The **rood stair** is still open; the 14th century **rood screen** has beautiful, delicate tracery; there's a very good two-decker Jacobean **pulpit** – and close at hand, fixed to the screen, an **hour glass stand** from days of long and ruminative sermons. On the wall beside the pulpit are details of a **memorial brass** of 1495 to William de Grey, here for eternity with two wives, 10 daughters and five sons. In the **chancel**, a lovely **double piscina** and three-seat **sedilia**; and around three sides of the **altar** (the only such arrangement in Norfolk) a splendid set of 17th century altar rails with 'barley sugar' balusters.

Necton
All Saints

map ref. E6

Topped by its cheerful lantern, the tower of All Saints is a splendid, powerful and richly composed expression of the high **Perpendicular** style of the 15th century – and it was wholly built in 1865! The rest of the building is true medieval, **Decorated** and Perpendicular. Inside, the glory of the church is its very fine roof, in which **hammerbeams** alternate with **arched braces**, and richly augmented by angels on the hammers. Some years ago this writer walked into All Saints to find work in progress on the roof – and was offered the wonderful chance to see something which, until discovered a few days before, had not been seen by human eyes for more than four centuries… a knot on the top of a beam, in the angle between roof and wall plates, was beautifully carved into a study of a mouse munching an acorn held between its forepaws. Truly a labour of love for God's eyes only.

Norwich St Peter Mancroft

map ref: K6

The great town church of Norwich, in the very heart of the old city, is a magnificent sight at any time. Floodlit at night, with the castle as backdrop, it has a drama of its own. The value of this impressive building is that it was raised in a concerted period of 25 years beginning in 1430, in a breathtaking example of the **Perpendicular** style, and is virtually unaltered from that time. Inside it is all space and light, under a lovely **hammerbeam** roof. Over the **font** – a **seven sacrament font** originally, but all the panels have been hacked away – is a remarkable 15th century canopy. Take a pair of binoculars to appreciate fully the east window: brought together here are some of the best surviving examples of Norwich painted glass of the 15th and 16th centuries.

Piscina and Sedilia

To the right of the altar in all medieval churches in past times, set into the south wall, were a piscina and sedilia, and many survive today. The piscina was in effect a sink – though a beautifully constructed and carved one – in which to wash the sacred vessels after the Mass. Water touching these vessels at once became hallowed; so the piscinas had a drain going directly down into the foundations, and thus into consecrated ground.

Occasionally one finds double piscinas, two side by side – one for the vessels, the other for the priest's hands. These enjoyed only a short popularity, and can be dated to about 1300-1320. Angle piscinas are set into the angle between wall and window, or wall and sedilia. This latter is a seat or set of seats (usually three) for the priests during long services.

Where the window embrasure has been let down to create the seats, it is known as a dropped sill sedilia. Where the seats are on different, descending levels, it is a graduated sedilia.

Richly carved canopies of the sedilia at Brisley St Bartholomew, page 13.

North Elmham St Mary

map ref. F4

Bishop Herbert de Losinga, who founded Norwich Cathedral in 1096, built the first church here at Elmham, and parts of it still remain, having survived rebuildings through several centuries. The late 14th century tower is impressive, and the whole composition of the building very handsome, with numerous interesting and intriguing details. The striking interior has **arcade** pillars and arches of the 13th century. Two hundred years later the **clerestory** was added, with its elegant **Tudor** windows. For the visitor to St Mary's, the bench ends and the screen are special attractions. The carved bench

ends present a jolly menagerie of odd birds and beasts, including a muzzled little fellow who presumably is a bear! At the **Reformation** the screen, with its panoply of saints, was pulled apart and the painted panels nailed face down to make floors for the pews. They were discovered during a 19th century restoration – and put back where they belong.

Pulham
St Mary

map ref. K9

St Mary's, a beautiful church overall, with a splendid 15th century tower and a lovely 13th century **chancel**, is especially renowned for its phenomenal 15th century **porch**. A glory of carving and ornamentation, it is of two storeys, topped off with a lushly carved, pierced parapet with pinnacles on which sit heraldic animals. An **Annunciation** scene fills the spandrels to each side of the entrance arch, and to each side of them is a charming frieze of angels playing musical instruments. Look for the carving of the wolf guarding the severed head of St Edmund,

King of East Anglia – part of the legend of Edmund's death at the hands of the Danes, when they shot his body full of arrows then lopped off his head and threw it into woodland. When the king's followers came, they found his body – but were called to the head by the wolf… who then followed the cortege to Bury St Edmunds.

Inside, the **rood screen** has its 15th century base: the upper part is Victorian (1886), and very well done. Upon the lower screen are painted images of the apostles, several of which can be recognised by their symbols – a boat for St Jude;

a fuller's club (like a hockey stick) for St James the Less; a chalice for St John; an X-cross for St Andrew; a scallop shell for St James the Great. The chancel has a fine, contemporary **double piscina** with interlaced arches. The striking **font** was re-coloured during the 1886 restoration. It is thought to be 15th century, and its carvings so sharp and fresh because it was for long covered over in plaster, which preserved it intact.

Ranworth
St Helen

map ref. M5

St Helen's is a church with a long story of disaster and recoveries, renowned for its welcome each year to many thousands of visitors, and famous for its glorious **rood screen**; its rare medieval cantor's (singer's) desk, seen in forefront of main picture; and its manuscript Antiphoner (sung verses in the daily offices or services) of 1400 (detail). The screen extends right across the church, and is complete with rare projections which would have contained **nave altars** before the **Reformation** as they do once again today. The craftsmanship of the whole screen is superb; its paintings acknowledged as among the finest in England. Among those paintings is a wonderful St Michael (picture right), winged, feathered, armed – and despatching a dragon with the casual air of one who does it every day before breakfast.

Salle St Peter and St Paul

map ref. H4

For Munro **Cautley**, the leading authority in the middle years of this century on Norfolk and Suffolk churches, it was 'the finest church in Norfolk, having examples of nearly everything that a church should have'. It has been called the Cathedral of the fields, standing clear in splendid isolation, a mighty church with a tower seen from miles around. It is the slimness of the tower in relation to its height – a height accentuated by its huge corner pinnacles – which astonishes the eye. We can date it pretty accurately too. Among the shields carved over the west door is the coat of arms of Henry V when he was Hal, Prince of Wales. Note too in the **spandrel** (the triangle over the arch of the door) the carved angel. He's covered with feathers which look like a tight fitting garment… because the carver had seen them like that in miracle plays of the time. Inside, the church is a serene splendour, with superb roofs flocking with angels; a **seven sacrament font** with the possibly unique addition below the bowl of angels bearing objects relating to the scenes above them; fine old carved medieval **misericordes**; and a splendid **three decker pulpit**. Give yourself time at Salle, and take a detailed guide book.

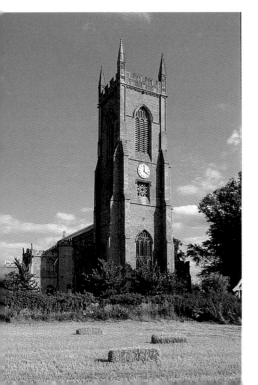

Pulpits and Hour Glasses

The part played by preaching varied considerably during the middle ages, but **pulpits** do not seem to have been commonly provided in parish churches before the 14th century. But when good preachers were around, the faithful responded, as Margery Kempe, King's Lynn's redoubtable 'religious woman', recorded in her dictated autobiography late in her life (she died about 1440). When a fine preacher came to Lynn 'how fast the pepyl cam rennyng to heryn the sermoun'. But another writer of the period was considerably more critical: 'Summe comuyn obstinat in there synne… Summe comyn only to heryn newe thyngis… Summe comyn only to be seyn'. What's new! More than 200 pre-Reformation pulpits

survive in England, with a good representation of them in Norfolk. The pulpit was seen as a platform for teaching – thus the favourite representations painted upon them of the **Four Latin Doctors**, the four great theologians and teachers of the early church (see Castle Acre, Burnham Norton and Horsham St Faiths in this book). The Reformation brought a great increase in preaching, with Edward VI charging church wardens to make sure they had 'a comely and honest pulpit' from which to preach God's word. Yet for all that very few of the clergy by all accounts were trusted to preach the reformed religion until the 17th century, when the pulpit became central to worship (see panel on Prayer Book interiors, page 95).

With this new era of preaching the **hour glass** came into its own. The stand in which the glass stood was either fixed onto the pulpit itself (see Wiggenhall St Germaine, page 102) or conveniently within reach (see Merton St Peter, page 66). The running of the sand through the hour glass really did take an hour. The English poet George Herbert, writing in Charles I's reign, probably spoke for all when he observed that 'the parson exceeds not an hour in preaching, because all ages have thought that a competency'. Still, there were those clerics who turned the glass over and started again… The hour glass in medieval stained glass and paintings carries another message – time's passage; death's inevitability; the vanity of human existence. Cheerful stuff!

Salthouse St Nicholas map ref. E8

From the ridge rising gently above it, St Nicholas's provides the centre point of a wonderful view of fields and shore and sea beyond. When the winds blow here they give no quarter as they pound everything in their way – which is why the windows of St Nicholas's are so narrow, as they hunch their shoulders against whatever the weather throws at them. It is all late **Perpendicular**, though the tracery in those 'hunched' windows suggests the **Decorated** style of nearly 200 years earlier. The building was completed in 1503 by Sir Henry Heydon, whose family exercised power for generations in this part of Norfolk. The interior, under **arch-braced** roofs, is fairly spartan, but nonetheless impressive for that. In the aisles the window openings drop down to make seats, an arrangement which can also be found in this part of the county at Cley and its neighbour, Wiveton, and also at Tunstead. These hark back to the times when most churches had no permanent seating – and 'the weak went to the wall'.

On display here is an interesting rarity from the reign of Elizabeth I. It's Bishop John Jewel's book *Defence of the Apologie of the Churche of England*, dating from about 1564, which around this time – by command of the Queen – became an obligatory book in all churches. For within it, so that the people might understand, was an explanation and defence of the theological position of the new Church of England, in the wake of the great break with Rome by Elizabeth's father, Henry VIII.

Shelton
St Mary

map ref. M5

St Mary's is one of those churches at which aficionados exclaim aloud in sheer pleasure – especially if the visit is on a day of bright sunshine, when this lovely building positively glows. Firstly, its style: the body of the church is superlative **Perpendicular**. Second, the building materials: red brick with stone dressings, which is

what makes the place so stunning under sunlight. The simple tower is earlier, being 14th century **Decorated**. But it has its own story to tell. To Shelton, when her life was in danger during the reign of 'Bloody Mary', came Princess Elizabeth, the future Elizabeth I – and in this very tower she took refuge. The interior is inspiringly bright and

light. There is some outstanding 15th/16th century glass here (see if you can spot the angel playing bagpipes); and a much altered tomb to Sir Robert Houghton (1623), seen in his judge's robes with his family. And don't miss the gorgeous **Royal Arms** of William III.

South Creake
St Mary
the Virgin

map ref. M5

A big, beautiful church, superbly maintained, where every day of the year seems to be a flower festival. The **chancel** is 13th century, the tower 14th century **Decorated**; and south **aisle** and **clerestory Perpendicular**. Note on the 14th century **porch** the crowned Ms for the Virgin Mary, picked out in stone and flint flushwork. Inside you could think that the **Reformation** had never

happened, with **rood**, side altars, votive saints and reserved sacrament suspended over the High **Altar** of Our Lady. These things are a long tradition here. Before the Reformation there were six side altars and 16 votive lights. But Protestant reforming zeal came nonetheless: look at the savagely defaced **seven sacrament font**; and at the **rood screen**, where all signs of the original

paintings have been gouged away. Look up at the angels in the **hammerbeam** roof. There was a village tradition that Cromwellian soldiers were billeted in the church – and used the angels for target practice. When the carvings were restored in 1958, lead shot was found embedded in the angels' wood-carved bodies. Folk memory was here proved wholly accurate.

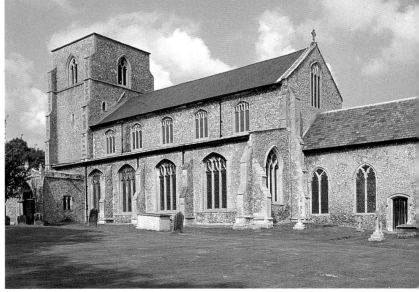

South Lopham St Andrew

map ref. K5

St Andrew's is justly celebrated for its magnificent **Norman** tower, the best architecture of the period in Norfolk save for Norwich Cathedral itself. Sir Nikolaus **Pevsner** dated it as 'no later than 1120'. It is a central tower, **nave** to one side, **chancel** to the other, and rears powerfully to a height of 100ft. Its detail is superb, from the muscular bell openings and down through its striking **blind** arcading. The attractive **Decorated** style lower window was inserted in the early 14th century. But St Andrew's was not a Norman foundation. Close to the filled-in nave north door there is, high up, a 'porthole' window which is typically **Saxon** (it has been dated as around 1010). Masses of interesting detail inside.

Swaffham St Peter and St Paul map ref. L2

Here we have the grand town church of a prosperous market town of the Middle Ages, renowned for its extremely beautiful double **hammerbeam** roof, clustered with angels… 192 of them! The building is largely **Perpendicular**, from the second half of the 14th century. The tower came afterwards, completed in about 1510 and built wholly in stone – a rarity in Norfolk. The pretty little spirelet, which can be seen for miles around in every direction, came considerably later, in 1897. The interior suggests vast space, with that wonderful roof at once compelling attention. Seek out a monument in the south **transept** to one Katherine Steward, died 1590 – she was the maternal grandmother of Oliver Cromwell. Don't miss the carvings on the prayer desk in the **chancel** of the Pedlar of Swaffham and his dog – and discover their magical story. As you'll learn, the Pedlar became rich, and built the north **aisle**. As you leave the church by the **porch**, look back. There on the gable is the Pedlar's faithful dog.

Terrington
St Clement

map ref. E8

St Clement's has been called The Cathedral of the Marshes, as well it might, for this vast **Perpendicular** church, rising majestically above its surrounding Fenlands, astounds by its size (it is 167 feet long) and seems almost unreal. The body of the church was designed to take a tower at a central crossing but, possibly because it would have been too risky, the huge bell tower we see today was raised up separately. This arrangement left the way clear for the mighty, five-**light** west window, set off by **crocketted** pinnacles on the gables above, and lovely figure niches under canopies to each side. The noble interior has much of interest, but its particular treasure is the wonderful 17th century **font cover**, which opens to show painted scenes of the life of Christ. We are poignantly reminded here of the tearing down of the 'popish' stone **altars** (or **mensa**) when the **Reformation** came to England in the reigns of Henry VIII and his son, the boy-king Edward VI. There are three such altar slabs, still with some of their **consecration crosses**, set into the floor beneath the crossing (above which the intended tower would have stood) and yet another one below the high altar.

Thompson
St Martin

map ref. L2

St Martin's, which dates largely from the 14th century, is a lovely, small church, set in quiet countryside, with an interior of serene beauty which is quite ravishing. The main picture here is looking westward from the sanctuary, giving a view in the foreground of the intriguing 17th century

communion rails with a 'lip' in the top rail. Was it to ledge books? Or could it have been, in a period when the communion bread was rough chunks of ordinary household bread, to catch stray crumbs should they chance to fall? Just out of sight to the left are a handsome **piscina** and **sedilia**:

from between the arches, three little **Green Men** peer out. Some of the stalls seen to each side have their ancient **misericordes**. The lovely wooden **screen** is 14th century; and the splendid **three-decker pulpit** 17th century Stuart work.

Thurning
St Andrew

map ref. M7

An unpretentious little church, tranquilly set – and equally tranquil inside. It is largely 14th century, as are the pretty contemporary windows in the **Decorated** style, facing the camera. In the east end is a beautiful **rectilinear** window from that same period, re-used from a long-gone **chancel**. Inside, time seems to have stopped long ago. There are **box pews** which all had their own allocations to the village pecking order; and pews for the hall and rectory servants. There's a big solid **three decker pulpit** – and hat pegs for the men and boys all along the south wall! – 'A place for every man, and every man in his place'.

Royal Arms and Decalogue Boards

Royal Arms – the coat of arms of the reigning monarch of the time – have been features of our churches since the time of Henry VIII.

With the Reformation instituted by Henry VIII and forcefully continued by his son, the boy-king Edward VI, all images and signs of 'popery' and 'superstition' were torn out and destroyed, in the name of Protestant reform. **Roods** (see feature panel on page 38) were destroyed and rood screens either destroyed or defaced. **Fonts** carved with saints or 'popish' images were ruthlessly vandalised. Walls were whitewashed to cover over the colours and imagery which were a natural part of medieval, Roman Catholic observance in this country.

When Elizabeth I came to the throne, compromise was the order of the day, although it veered towards Protestantism. Where the rood had been, within the curve of the chancel arch, she commanded that this

space – the tympanum – should be filled in with boards and her Royal Arms painted there. This enforced the fact that she, Elizabeth, was Supreme Governor of the Church of England.

At Ludham St Catherine her Arms can be seen in place in the chancel arch; likewise at Tivetshall St Margaret. At Kenninghall St Mary the Arms have been moved from that position, but may still be seen. Fine examples from other reigns in Norfolk are at Little Snoring – a rare set for James II, who reigned only three years; Stow Bedon – a magnificent set for Charles II; Great Witchingham – another good Charles II; Shelton – a beauty for William III; and at Upwell, a vast and splendid Arms for Queen Victoria.

At Tivetshall the composition for Elizabeth offers a variation on the theme – not only are her Arms sumptuously displayed, but the Ten Commandments appear also. This leads

us to the **Decalogue Board**, a large board upon which the Ten Commandments are written, which stems from another of Elizabeth's commands.

In 1560 she ordered her Archbishop of Canterbury, Matthew Parker – born in Norwich and one of its most famous sons – to see 'that the tables of the Commandments be comely set or hung up in the east end of the chancel'. Not long afterwards came another order: the decalogues must be fixed to the east wall of the church, over the communion table (the altar).

In some cases the tympanum over the chancel arch was filled not with the Royal Arms, but with decalogue boards which might include also the Lord's Prayer and other 'comfortable words'. Today the decalogues in most cases have been moved from their east end and chancel arch positions, and set up elsewhere in the church.

Trunch St Botolph

map ref. M5

A neat building, with its tall, trim tower complemented by a high **nave** under a pitched lead roof. It is all **Perpendicular**, though the graceful traceries suggest the earlier style of **Decorated**. Just off the top picture to the right is an unusual feature, shared in Norfolk only with Warham St Mary – the **priest's door** into the **chancel** has a little porch over it, with a buttress on top. There is much to enjoy inside, but the moment we walk in one thing captures our attention and admiration: St Botolph's magnificent oak **font canopy**, only one of four in England, including the one at St Peter Mancroft in Norwich. It stands around the elegant 15th century font on six posts joined by flattened arches: above them sits a wonderfully rich canopy. All is riotously carved with flowers, birds, animals – including monkeys and a pig wearing a bishop's mitre! – and a wild man fighting a dragon. The choir stalls in the chancel are covered in carved graffiti – and bored through to take ink wells. Reason: a school was held here around 1700. Take a closer look at the timbering on which the stalls stand. It is raised up, and carved through with little openings. The idea was to make a sounding box to give resonance to the choir's singing. A medieval amplification system, so to speak!

Low Side Windows

Low Side Windows are a fascinating feature of medieval churches whose purpose has long been matter for debate. They are almost always found low in the south wall of the chancel, close to the chancel arch. Sometimes they are separate, small windows; more often the lower section of a larger window; but always fitted with shutters so that they could be opened.

So what were they for? One theory is that they were for lepers, who could receive the Mass through the open windows – overlooking the fact that in medieval England the movements of lepers were strictly controlled. Another view is that penitents would kneel outside and make confession to a priest seated inside.

Another idea is that the window provided extra light for a special altar, though this seems unlikely. Fourthly, and probably much more accurate, is that at the high point of the Mass, when the priest raised the Host (the bread) an assistant rang a handbell through the opened window.

In that moment the villagers going about their business could stop for a moment, cross themselves, and thus share in the Mass.

Prayer Book Interiors

Wilby All Saints, Warham St Mary and Bylaugh St Mary are three churches given special mention in the introduction to this book (page xiii) as well as their own 'portrait' entries (pages 106-7, 100-1 and 18 respectively). All have in common that they have **Prayer Book interiors**.

Before the Reformation church interiors were splendid with colour on walls, capitals, mouldings, statues, hangings and windows. But after 1549 churches were stripped of their colour and imagery, walls and screens whitewashed, and complete refurnishing enforced. From the 17th century, this meant low communion tables, communion rails, **three decker pulpits** and **box pews**. These Prayer Book churches survived until the 19th century when the Victorians turned against them. In the 1840s the High Church movement campaigned for the re-introduction of ancient ritual, and the replacement of the simple beauty of these interiors with pseudo-medieval ones. So most of the Prayer Book examples were swept away to make way for the typical furnishings we see today.

Wall Paintings

Wall paintings are precious things in England's medieval churches – so many were covered over or destroyed at the time of the **Reformation** and in the **Puritan period** in the 17th century that those which remain are both scarce and fragile. The vast majority of those which do survive belong to the 14th and 15th centuries, though some date from the 11th century. There were none recorded from that period in Norfolk until an amazing find in 1996 in the ruined church of St Mary the Virgin at Houghton-on-the-Hill, near Swaffham.

Bob Davey, churchwarden of nearby South Pickenham, found the church while out walking. It was ruinous, overwhelmed by ivy and in an overgrown jungle of a church-yard. But worse, when he managed to get into the building, he found evidence that it had been used by satanists. He at once set to work to clear churchyard and ivy-clad walls and, somehow, to restore the church. Then paintings came to light under rotting plaster. Experts were called in – and they dated some of what they found to 1090, three years after the death of William the

Conqueror. Yet more exciting, they discovered a depiction of the Holy Trinity which was thought not to have been in widespread use in European church art until the 15th century.

As work began to discover what more secrets St Mary's might hold, English Heritage provided funds to build a new roof and Norfolk County Council helped undertake structural reinforcements and extra weather proofing.

Now we know that on top of the 11th century paintings are 13th century paintings on plaster applied at that time. And that over the 13th century work is a layer of 17th century biblical texts and **decalogues**. A few years ago there was another exciting find here in Norfolk, at St Faith's, Little Witchingham, again semi-ruinous and overgrown. What came to light there was a quite remarkable series of 'framed' pictures which suggested that originally almost the whole church had been covered in these 'visual lessons'. Dating from the first half of the 14th century, they included a fascinating 'comic strip' of 13 scenes of what seems to

be a Passion cycle – that is, the Crucifixion of Christ and the events leading up to it. In addition, there are vestiges of a St Christopher and a St George scene.

St Christopher is perhaps the commonest of all representations in wall paintings. He is the patron saint of travellers, who was almost always painted opposite the entrance door of the church. Thus one could open the door, see him, cross oneself with holy water – and be safe from all harm that day. There are huge Christopher images at Crostwight, Wickhampton, Seething and Heydon (plus fine fragments of a range of subjects); a wonderful set of scenes from his life at Hemblington; a fragment at Edingthorpe; and vestiges at Belton and Haddiscoe. Wickhampton has one of the finest ranges of 14th century wall paintings in England. Apart from Christopher, there are two favourite 'improving story' cartoons of the period and a Resurrection of Christ. Heydon has another fine series, but not so identifiable. Other Norfolk churches with wall paintings worth a visit are Haddiscoe, Potter Heigham, Attleborough and Belton.

Walpole
St Peter

map ref. E8

Here we are deep in the region of the great Fenland churches, so beloved of the Prince of Wales, who is a particular enthusiast for Norfolk churches. St Peter's is said to be his favourite. As Terrington St Clement is called The Cathedral of the Marshes, so this vast and glorious building is The Queen of the Marshes. It is all **Perpendicular** splendour, with superb **porches** and huge windows at the height of the style which flood the interior with light. Beautiful soaring **arcade** pillars punctuate the **nave**, whose centre-point is an immense chandelier of brass and wrought iron,

of a size in ratio to its surroundings, which was brought here nearly 200 years ago. Notice the unusual arrangement in the south **aisle** of pews – a mix of 15th and 17th century work – raised at different levels and looking inwards. In the magnificent chancel, a memorable gothic masterpiece, don't miss the 15th century stalls which have camels carved on the ends. Nor the arm rests carved with the wolf holding the head of Edmund, East Anglia's king and martyr. Their wonderful legend is told in the entry on Pulham St Mary on page 74.

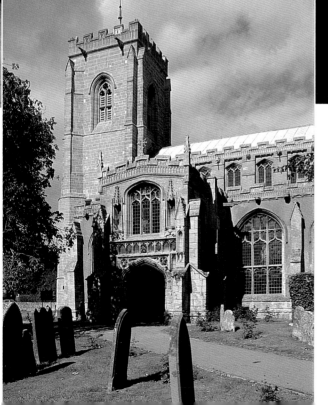

West Walton
St Mary

map ref. E6

To visit St Mary's for the first time is a special occasion for any enthusiast for English churches. For quite simply this is one of the best **Early English** churches in the kingdom, built all of a piece, including its separate tower, around 1240. 'Of the thousands of churches I have seen', declared the leading authority Munro **Cautley**, 'this is the finest example of early 13th century work'. Half a century on, we have no cause to question his judgement. The tower, standing clear of the church, is in a class apart, even by Norfolk's standards. Inside the church, the perfection of form is breathtaking. One can but say: go and experience it for yourself.

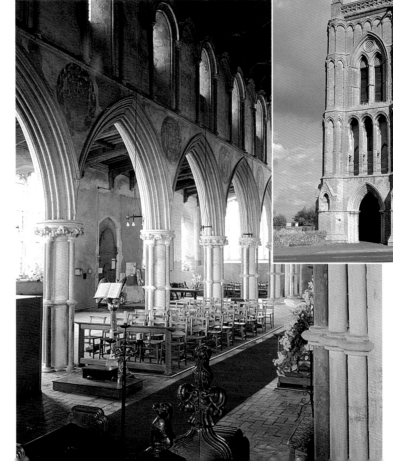

Worstead
St Mary

map ref. E6

Worstead is the village which gave its name to the famous woollen cloth. In turn, wool wealth in the second half of the 14th century (for St Mary's was completed in one continuous 20 year campaign begun in 1379) paid for this fine pile. It is acknowledged to be one of the best churches of its period in the county. It is marked by its superb tower, thrusting to 109ft, and by confident, powerful **Perpendicular** lines throughout. The interior is grand and open, and crowned by a fine **hammerbeam** and **arch-braced** roof. Of special interest is the chancel **rood screen** (dated 1512) which is enormously high at nearly 18ft. Among its painted saints it has **William of Norwich**, holding nails and a dagger; and Uncumber, who miraculously grew a long beard to make herself ugly in the sight of an unwanted suitor and to escape a fate worse than death! A fine set of 18th century oak **box pews** look well in this spacious setting. The elegant eight-sided **font** on its three steps (the top one in the form of a cross) has the beautiful remains of a soaring cover of medieval origin, which was restored in the 1950s.

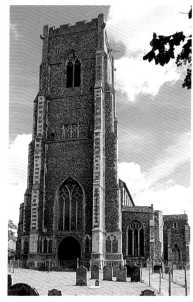

Warham
St Mary

map ref. M5

On the face of it, this is a small, unpretentious village church – but it has much to offer. Until a few years ago the tower was accepted by all authorities to be 14th century **Decorated**. Then restoration and repointing work revealed, just below the belfry openings, the outlines – three on each side – of filled-in 'porthole' windows of typically **Saxon** style. The **chancel** has a delightful curiosity which St Mary's shares only with Trunch St Botolph – a **priest's door** over which is a little porch, from which springs a buttress. The interior has a lovely surprise: a **Prayer Book** arrangement of furnishings which, though not installed until 1800-1, takes us back to the world of 18th century

Protestantism and two and a half centuries of
prayer book worship. High **box pews**, a splendid
three-decker pulpit and what Sir John Betjeman
called 'a bird bath font', help create in this simple
building an atmosphere and seemliness which are
quietly memorable.

Wiggenhall St Germans St Germaine

map ref. F4

A pretty riverside church is St Germaine's with a slim tower solidly buttressed at its 13th century base (note the long pencil **lancet** window of the period in the second storey) and neatly added to in stone in the 15th century. The homely brick porch is 16th century. The **clerestory** windows have basket arches – their shape is self-explanatory. When you go inside look at the tower arch – it's 13th century with dog-tooth moulding. The finely carved **pulpit**, dated 1631, is complete with its **hour glass** and stand, an evocative left-over from days of very long sermons. The benches are 15th century with abundantly carved ends, ranging from little figures in the dress of the day to lively studies of the vices: Avarice clutches his money bags; Lust clutches a mildly surprised lady; and Gluttony pours more wine.

Here Lyes ſtone Be bold to Tell
One that dyed and lived as well
Who ſcarſe left her Paralell

That dyed old and lived not long
Very weake and wondrous ſtrong
one would Take and doe no wrong

Here oh here lyesrhetMe ſee
Vertue In Epitome
Part of heauens Eternitye

Summer fruits that Ripen faſt
Very rarely long doe laſt
Choyceſt flowers fade with Ablaſt

ſacred to the Memory
Of Moores Laſt Child Dorothy
Who halfe Fiue Yeares Changed hur Life
And Died Wright of Waynforts Wife
Dyed as you and I Muſt doe
Sixteene Hundred Sixty two

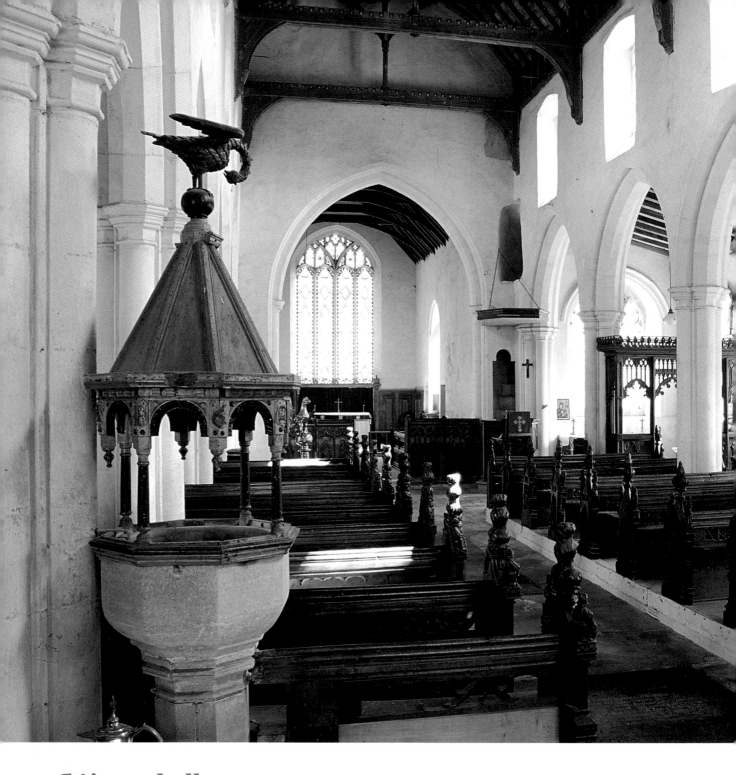

Wiggenhall
St Mary
St Mary the
Virgin

map ref. K9

A largely 15th century church, with an interior of appealing simplicity and light and airy spaciousness. The plain yet graceful **font** has an attractive **Jacobean** cover (dated 1625) on the top of which is a rather fine **pelican in her piety**. Below the **chancel arch** is the base of the 15th century **screen**, painted with eight saints. In front of it, a large brass eagle lectern, carrying the date 1518. In the south **aisle** is the opulent and imposing tomb of Sir Henry Kirvil, who died in 1624, the last of his line. But the family went out with style. He is in full armour, and his lady fashionably gowned in farthingale (a skirt worn

over hoops) and rich cloak and hood.

Now to St Mary's early 16th century pews, one of the most complete sets in Norfolk and ranking with the best in England. They are carved with an amazing array of saints. Among these are several of the Virgin Saints who in the Middle Ages inspired enormous devotional zeal – like St Agatha, seen here with a knife suspended over her bared breast. She was the daughter of a wealthy family in 6th century Sicily. The pagan consul was determined to seduce her, but she remained stubbornly chaste. In revenge he had her horribly tortured, dragged through fire – and

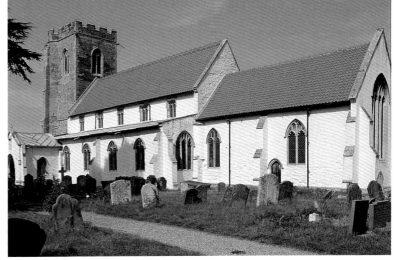

her breasts cut off. Thus she is invoked against fire and against diseases of the breasts – and is patron saint of bell-founders…

Now, among so many holy figures, seek out the man with a beehive! He's almost certainly St Ambrose – one of the **Four Latin Doctors**. The beehive recalls the story that, when he was a baby, a swarm of bees settled on his cradle and hovered over his lips – a divine foretelling of the future eloquence which would be his. In truth he turned out to be a mighty preacher, whose words tamed even the bloodthirsty Roman emperors of his era in the 4th century.

Wilby
All Saints

map ref. M5

All Saints is a handsome building of fine proportions, its 14th century **Decorated** tower standing out in the surrounding countryside. The body of the church is largely Decorated, with especially fine windows both at the west end, and in the east end of the lovely **chancel**. But the real reason for coming to Wilby, and remembering it thereafter with pleasure, is the outcome of a fire which happened here in 1633. In its wake came a complete refurnishing in the **Prayer Book** fashion: a **three decker pulpit**; a west gallery and

ringing chamber, from which one looks down the full length of the building; benches, **box pews**; and – both of lovely, homely carpenter's work – tall gates into the chancel and **communion rails** with a neat little gate in ratio. Over the door is a particularly splendid set of **Royal Arms** for Charles I – was it hidden after the King's judicial murder by Cromwell's men, and brought back at the Restoration? There is much more to see at All Saints, so give yourself time, with a good guide book in hand.

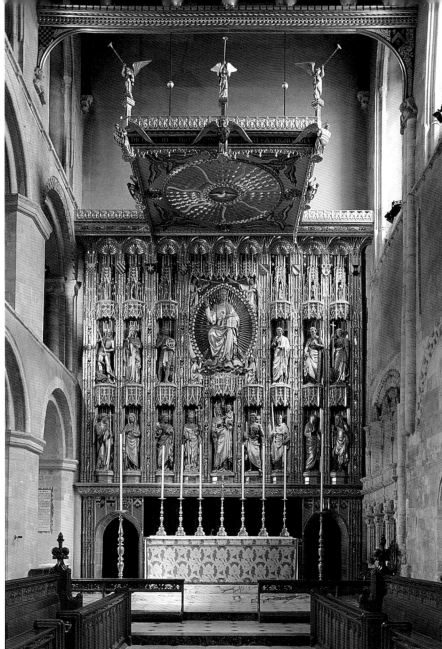

Wymondham St Mary and St Thomas of Canterbury

map ref. H4

Wymondham Abbey at first sight is both a splendour – and a puzzle. Mighty square tower at one end; romantic ruin of another at the east. It requires a long and tempestuous tale and more space than we have here, to tell of 300 years of enmity, bickering and fighting between priory monks and Wymondham townsfolk; of the row getting so bad that it went to the Pope himself in Rome for judgement; and of bitter separation of the warring parties. When the Dissolution came, the monks lost all – and the townsfolk kept what was theirs. Inside, the ancient meets the modern:

Norman architectural power, crowned by a glorious 15th century **hammerbeam** roof alive with angels; and in the east end a glowing, vast and awesome reredos created in 1919 by Sir Ninian Comper. It's said that in 1912 Comper had acquired an all-consuming passion for the Ballet Russe during their second London season and was influenced by the colouring and éclat of the sets designed by Leon Bakst – hence the elaborate glory and theatrical drama of Wymondham's reredos.

Glossary

Aisle Extension along the north and/or south sides of the nave; and in larger churches, occasionally to the chancel.

Altar See feature panel on altars, page 37.

Anchorite See Julian (Mother Julian of Norwich).

Annunciation When the Archangel Gabriel came down to the Virgin Mary with the news that she would bear the Christ-child.

Arcades Range of arches supported on columns/pillars.

Archbrace See feature panel on roofs, page 59.

Assumption The Virgin Mary's carrying up into Heaven, body and soul.

Aumbrey See feature panel on aumbries, page 37.

Bar tracery Bar tracery developed from plate tracery. Plate tracery was sculpted directly through one piece of stone. Bar tracery was made up of separate pieces of stone, giving greater flexibility of design.

Black Death The great plague of 1349-50, which killed a third of the national population, and probably half of Norfolk's. See entry on reticulated tracery in feature panel on architectural styles of windows, page 21.

Boss Centre projection which locks the ribs in vaulted roofs, often richly carved.

Box pews Pews contained within high wooden surrounds. See feature panel on Prayer Book interiors, page 95.

Brasses See feature panel on brasses, page 37.

Blind arcading Raised outlines of arches as decorative feature on walls.

Butterfly headdress A headdress fashionable in mid-15th century. A gauze veil supported on a wire frame extended outwards from the head like butterfly wings.

Canopy of Honour A painted section of the roof over the altar or the rood.

Capitals Carved top of a pillar, separating pillar from arch.

Cautley, Munro Leading expert in the middle years of this century on Norfolk and Suffolk churches; author of two authoritative books on the subject.

Chancel The east-end section of a church, containing the altar, choir stalls etc. See feature panel on page 37.

Chantry/Guild Chapels Before the Reformation, many churches contained numerous private chapels, ministered to by their own priests. Chantries were created and paid for by private individuals/families; Guilds by trade/religious guilds, the medieval equivalent of 20th century 'friendly societies' and trades unions.

Chequerwork Decorative mix of stone or brick with flint in chess board pattern.

Clerestory Range of windows above nave to admit extra light, thus 'clear-storey'.

Collar of S's A 15th century mark of high royal favour. See background on Ashwellthorpe All Saints in introduction, page xi.

Consecration Cross See feature panel on altars, page 37.

Corbel Support set in wall to carry weight from above.

Credence Shelf Shelf within piscina, to carry sacred vessels. See feature panel on piscinas, page 71.

Crocket Exuberantly carved decoration in form of flowers/leaves etc on spires and pinnacles.

Decalogues See feature panel on Royal Arms, page 92.

Early English See feature panel on architectural styles of windows, page 21.

Easter Sepulchre See concluding part of introduction, page xvi.

Fonts See feature panel on page 16.

Four Latin Doctors See feature panel on pulpits, page 80.

Gargoyles Waterspouts, usually carved in animal/devilish form, to throw water away from roofs and walls. See introduction, page x.

Geometric Style during Decorated period. See feature panel on architectural styles of windows, page 21.

Green Man Pagan image, symbol of fertility, absorbed into Christianity. Human face from which grow tendrils and leaves.

Guild Chapels See chantry chapels.

Hammerbeams See feature panel on roofs, page 59.

Hatchments Lozenge shaped frames bearing the coat of arms of a dead person, made for his/her funeral, and finding a place subsequently in his/her parish church.

Hour glass See feature panel on pulpits, page 80.

Instruments of the Passion Items associated with Christ's Crucifixion – cross, Crown of Thorns, spear which pierced His side; vinegar, and reed and sponge by which it was administered; dice used to cast lots for His clothing; and the ladder.

Jacobean Style relating to reign of James I, 1603-25.

Julian Mother Julian of Norwich. Celebrated 14th century holy woman who lived as an anchorite – walled into a cell, where she prayed, wrote and gave wise advice via a small window to those who consulted her.

Kennel Headdress A style of headdress fashionable in the opening decades of the 16th century. It had a pointed arch over the forehead, with borders down each side of the face.

Lancet See feature panel on architectural styles of windows, page 21.

Lenten Veil A dark veil hung across the chancel in pre-Reformation times to curtain off the high altar during Lent.

Lights This can refer to the candles burning before side altars; or to the number of divisions in a window between the mullions (uprights).

Long and short work A typical Saxon form of work at corners of buildings, with long uprights alternating with flat slabs or stones.

Low side window See feature panel on page 95.

Lych-gate Gateway into a churchyard, originally specifically to rest the coffin on the way to the funeral. From the Anglo-Saxon lych, meaning corpse.

Mensa slabs See feature panel on altars, page 37.

Misericordes Stalls with hinged seats, under which are often irreverent and humorous carvings.

Monstrance Decorative container in which to display the sacrament to worshippers.

Mouchette A curved dagger shape used in the 14th century Decorated period of architecture.

Mullions The uprights in the traceries of windows.

Napped Flints Flints split through the middle, and the flat surface set outwards in mortar.

Nave The main body of the church, from the Latin *navis*, a ship.

Nine Orders of Angels See background to St Michael and All Angels, Barton Turf, in introduction, page xii.

Norman See feature panel on architectural styles of windows, page 21.

North Doors See feature panel on porches, page 9.

Ogee A flowing S-shape, introduced in the 14th century, used in tracery etc.

Parclose Screen A screen closing off a side chapel from the rest of the church.

Pelican in her piety A repeated symbol in Christian imagery. The legend tells that the pelican killed its young in a surge of anger – then, 'on the third day', tore her own breast with her beak and the falling blood brought her young back to life. Thus Christ shed His blood and rose on the third day, to save mankind.

Perpendicular See feature panel on architectural styles of windows, page 21.

Pevsner, Sir Nikolaus Creator and writer of the remarkable *Buildings of England* series, 46 volumes, 1951-74, detailing the country's most notable buildings. His Norfolk volumes were published in 1992. An update on the North-East Norfolk volume by Dr W. Wilson appeared 1997.

Piscina See feature panel on page 71.

Plate Tracery See bar tracery.

Poppyheads Carved floral shape on heads of bench ends.

Porches See feature panel on page 9.

Prayer Book Churches See feature panel on prayer book interiors, page 95.

Priest's door Priest's separate entrance into chancel.

Pulpit See feature panel on page 80.

Puritan period Period of The Commonwealth and the ascendancy of Oliver Cromwell, following judicial killing of Charles I (January 30, 1649).

Reformation In England, Henry VIII's break with Rome, his proclamation (1534) as head of the English Church, and the establishment of the Protestant Church of England.

Reticulated See architectural styles of windows, page 21.

Rood See feature panel on roods/rood screens etc, page 38.

Royal Arms See feature panel on page 92.

Among many fine Royal Arms in Norfolk churches is this dashing set for Charles II at Great Witchingham. It was given by Oliver Le Neve – a member of an ancient Norfolk landed family – in 1660. It must have been his son who, 38 years later, was to bring some celebrity to the family when, in a duel he did not want to fight, he killed the overbearing, high and mighty Sir Henry Hobart of Blickling Hall.

St Christopher images See feature panel on wall paintings, page 95.

St William of Norwich In Holy Week 1144 a Norwich apprentice boy, William, was alleged to have been ritually killed by Jews on Mousehold Heath, adjoining the city. It provided a useful, money-making saint for the cathedral priory; and an excuse for a purge against the city's Jewish population. Modern scholarship accepts that the local Jews were wholly innocent.

Saxon See feature panel on architectural styles of windows on page 21.

Scratch Dials See feature panel on page 38.

Sedilia See feature panel on piscinas and sidilia on page 71.

Seven Acts of Mercy A subject of wall paintings and Christian example. The gospel of St Matthew commends – give food to the hungry and drink to the thirsty; make strangers welcome, clothe the naked, visit the sick, visit prisoners; and bury the dead.

Spandrel Triangular space over the arch of doors etc, in the angle between roofs and braces, often filled with decorative carving.

Squint An opening through a wall from a side altar, giving a view of the high altar, so that the Host (the bread – Christ's body) could be raised simultaneously at both altars.

Talbot Heraldic/architectural term for carved dogs placed atop the corners of porches etc.

Transept An outward extension to north or south from the body of a church, or from a central tower. See also aisles.

Tudor In architecture, high point of the Perpendicular style. See feature panel on architectural styles of windows.

Tympanum Arched space over a door, or across the width of an arch.

For example, see feature panel on Royal Arms on page 92.

Wall Paintings See feature panel on page 95.

With the discovery of remarkable medieval wall paintings in the ruined church of St Mary the Virgin at Houghton-on-the-Hill, scholars are having to re-assess the history of mural art in English churches.

Wall Plates See feature panel on roofs on page 59.

Wafer Oven Small ovens, set into a wall of the church, used to make wafers for the Mass.

Bibliography and further reading list

Carr, JL (foreword) *Churches in Retirement.* Redundant Churches Fund/HMSO, 1990.

Cautley, H Munro *Norfolk Churches.* Boydell Press, 1979 (facsimile of 1949 edition).

Chatfield, Mark *Churches the Victorians Forgot.* Moorland Publishing, 1989.

Cox, JC *The Parish Churches of England.* Batsford, 1950.

Duffy, Eamon *The Stripping of the Altars: Traditional Religion in England 1400-1580.* Yale University Press, 1992.

Fawcett, Richard *The Architecture and Furnishings of Norfolk Churches.* The Norfolk Society, 1974.

Horne, Dom Ethelbert *Scratch Dials.* Simpkin Marshall, 1929.

Macklin, HW *Monumental Brasses.* Swan Sonnenschein, 1891.

Mortlock, DP and Roberts, CV *The Popular Guide to Norfolk Churches.* 3 vols. Acorn Editions, 1981-85.

Nichols, Ann Elijenholm *Seeable Signs: The Iconography of the Seven Sacraments 1350-1544.* Boydell Press, 1994.

Pevsner, Nikolaus *Buildings of England series, N.E. Norfolk and Norwich; N.W. and S. Norfolk,* Penguin, 1962.

Robinson, JM *Treasures of the English Churches.* Sinclair-Stevenson, 1995.

Woodforde, Christopher *The Norwich School of Glass Painting in the 15th Century.* OUP, 1950.

Yaxley, Susan *The Reformation in Norfolk Parish Churches.* Larks Press, 1990.